The Abiding Disciple

A Blueprint for Your Life in Christ

Nate Sweeney

Sermon To Book
www.sermontobook.com

The Abiding Disciple / Nate Sweeney
ISBN-13: 978-1-952602-06-1

I want to dedicate this book to anyone who would dare to take on the joy of personal abandonment and absolute trust in following Christ. I pray that on your journey, this book will be a catalyst that pushes you into proximity with Christ, where transformation happens.

CONTENTS

Sacred Responsibility

If God created man in His image and likeness (Genesis 1:26) and placed man in a perfect environment, as the Bible tells us, then humans, like God, are spirit beings. We have souls, which include the mind, will, and emotions. God gave us physical bodies to house our spirits and souls while we are here on earth.

In the beginning, God created Adam and Eve, the first humans, and gave them many freedoms and fellowshipped with them on a regular basis. The only thing that was off limits was the tree of the knowledge of good and evil. God warned them never to partake of this tree because if they did, they would surely experience the consequence of death.

Things were great until Satan—a rebellious, fallen angel now disguised as a serpent—questioned God's motives and thereby deceived Adam and Eve into partaking of the forbidden tree in direct rebellion against God. When Adam and Eve disobeyed God, sin was released into the entire human race.

Because God is perfect and holy, sin now separated man from God. Adam's and Eve's choice broke God's heart, and He removed His beloved creation from the garden. Sin has produced depravity in every human since.

Only God can bring the restoration we need. Throughout human history, we see God pursuing us and drawing us into relationship with Him. God's ultimate plan was to send His only Son, Jesus Christ, to earth as God in the form of man (Philippians 2:5–11) to lay down His life for humanity through the shedding of blood. Jesus consumed God's wrath toward sin when He died on the cross and then conquered death through His resurrection. In Christ, we can have redemption from the wrath of God, and this free gift offers us a restored life in a relationship with Christ.

For all believers, whether we have been believers a long time or we are new to the faith, the difference between living a healthy spiritual life and living as a spiritual vagabond rests in our ability to cultivate and live in an intimate, abiding relationship with Christ. He will lead us into a deep understanding of Scripture, and then we will mature in Him as we walk with Him in personal experiences. Additionally, we will have fruits of transformation that will allow us to make some key investments in the lives of others and fulfill our sacred responsibility as disciples of Jesus to help others on their journeys with Him.

To help those who may not know how to have a rich life in Christ, I want to share some Scriptures that outline the salvation message. Salvation is not just an escape from hell and an eventual ticket to heaven. Eternal life in Christ begins now. When you accept Christ, your nature is changed, and your father is God instead of Satan. The Bible tells us that we are translated from the kingdom of darkness into His marvelous light (Colossians 1:13–14).

Our nature of depravity that causes us so many problems is reborn, and we are free to live as children of God instead of slaves to sin.

If you have repented of your sin and accepted Christ's payment for your sin, you have been born again:

> *For this reason we also, since the day we heard it, do not cease to pray for you, and to ask that you may be filled with the knowledge of His will in all wisdom and spiritual understanding; that you may walk worthy of the Lord, fully pleasing Him, being fruitful in every good work and increasing in the knowledge of God; strengthened with all might, according to His glorious power, for all patience and longsuffering with joy; giving thanks to the Father who has qualified us to be partakers of the inheritance of the saints in the light. He has delivered us from the power of darkness and conveyed us into the kingdom of the Son of His love, in whom we have redemption through His blood, the forgiveness of sins.*
>
> **—Colossians 1:9–14**

Because sin entered the human race, every person will partake of the depravity and sin against God. If you have ever lied, then you are a liar. If you have ever cheated, then you are a cheater. If you have harbored anger in your heart, the Bible says that you will be subject to judgment (Matthew 5:21–22). We all are guilty, "…for all have sinned and fall short of the glory of God" (Romans 3:23).

As stated above, we all have sinned, and the wages of sin are spiritual death and eternal separation from God: "For the wages of sin is death, but the gift of God is eternal life in Christ Jesus our Lord" (Romans 6:23).

God's love for you is so amazing that He offered the greatest gift He could. Would you be willing to give the most important thing in your life for someone who rejects you and doesn't care about your precious gift? I would not be able to do that, but God did: "For God so loved the world that He gave His only begotten Son, that whoever believes in Him should not perish but have everlasting life" (John 3:16).

The gateway to salvation is as easy as responding to God in faith as a direct result of your belief in your heart. You must believe that Christ paid the penalty for your sin and receive that by faith. Confession is a verbal declaration of what you believe in your heart. You are choosing by your own free will to accept the gift of God in Christ Jesus. (We will see more about this in chapter 5.)

After salvation, there is a lifetime of transformation that God does in you, but the first step is salvation:

> ...if you confess with your mouth the Lord Jesus and believe in your heart that God has raised Him from the dead, you will be saved. For with the heart one believes unto righteousness, and with the mouth confession is made unto salvation.
>
> **—Romans 10:9-10**

Salvation is a free gift from God. Your works are not good enough to save you. God said that our works of righteousness "are like filthy rags" (Isaiah 64:6). Grace is God's unmerited and undeserved favor. He gave it freely, and you must receive it free and clear of your works. By emphasizing your works, you feed your human nature instead of receiving His love and grace toward you: "For by grace you have been saved through faith, and that not of yourselves; *it is* the gift of God, not of works, lest anyone should boast" (Ephesians 2:8–9).

The love of Christ is the perfect balance of grace and truth: "And the Word became flesh and dwelt among us, and we beheld His glory, the glory as of the only begotten of the Father, full of grace and truth" (John 1:14). Many people fall into a ditch on either side of this and offer one or the other. Love offers grace for sins committed and truth to help you stay free from walking in that sin again. If you have grace without truth, you excuse people from the consequence of sin and the accountability of God's Word. If you offer truth without grace, you make love about laws and regulations that keep people in bondage: "I'll love you if you do this or don't do that." We need the balance of grace and truth to walk in the love of Christ.

What Just Happened?

After following that simple plan of salvation, when a person comes to know Christ, there are steps that the Bible gives to help the believer understand his or her newly found life in Him and build a solid foundation that will last. (For further information, you may find the plan "Knowing Christ and Making Him Known" on www.bible.com a helpful resource.)[1] Many new believers struggle without this knowledge and are not invited into a healthy platform of discipleship within a local biblical community that helps them along the way.

The lack of a solid foundation stunts a believer's growth and may even cause a new believer to fall by the wayside, living in constant doubt as to what has taken place in his or her life. Jesus said, "Most assuredly, I say to you, unless one is born again, he cannot see the kingdom of God" (John 3:3).

Many new believers wake up the day after they gave their hearts to Christ and ask themselves if what they did was real or just an emotional experience. Some are excited about digging into the Word and loving and serving God with their whole hearts.

Giving your heart to Christ is the most important decision you could ever make. The greatest thing God ever gave you was your individual free will. You are free to accept God or reject God, and He will honor your choice because He does not want slaves but creatures of willing obedience. He wants you to serve Him because you have accepted His love and received the gift that He gave in His Son, Jesus Christ. After accepting His love and the gift of His Son, we show our love in return by praising Him for what He has done and will do in our lives.

As new or established believers, we desire to grow deeper in the grace that God gives us and experience the boundless love that He offers us. For the established believer who is discipling a new believer, this book consists of a brief overview of the gospel message with strong, foundational investments to help establish a person's new life in Christ.

It is imperative to new believers that they be strengthened in their faith and given the milk of the Word of God. The Bible makes the comparison between a physical newborn baby and a spiritual one (1 Peter 2:2) because they both need a great deal of attention and care. This should take place in a biblical community where they can be nurtured and cared for as they develop into the life that Christ has for them.

A little baby left to fend for itself will not live long. Likewise, if newborn Christians are left to try to figure out their spiritual lives for themselves, they will not grow and mature very much. That is not the way God designed His family to operate. He created a blueprint for us to follow, and He gave us mature believers to encourage and exhort us.

Therefore, if anyone is in Christ, he is a new creation; old things have passed away; behold, all things have become new.

—2 Corinthians 5:17

However, if you are a new believer in Christ, you probably have many emotions swirling around and a lot of questions, and perhaps you are looking for a place to learn about how to grow in Christ. There is a wealth of information to learn in the Bible about life in Christ, and it will take a lifetime for you to grow into all that God has for you. It's okay to take your time and grow at a steady pace.

Below is an overview of the investments we will explore throughout this book:

- Abide in Christ

- What Is a Disciple?

- Self-Feeding on God's Word

- Introduction to the Holy Spirit

- Lifestyle of Repentance

- Transformation Versus Conformation

- Help on Your Journey

- God's Blueprint for Your Life

- Knowing Christ and Making Him Known

Please take your time in the study of this book to allow God to minister to you through its pages. This book is meant to be simple and easy to follow, requiring only a small time commitment. So many times, we begin a journey with huge expectations of what will be accomplished, and we bite off more than we can chew, leaving us so discouraged that we eventually quit the race. This book is specifically designed in a simple and short format to help avoid those pitfalls of discouragement.

I encourage you to take your life in Christ a few

minutes at a time, and eventually you will be running your race with joy in leaps and bounds. Give over the next season of your life to building a strong foundation in Christ.

Workbook Sections with a Journal Prompt

At the end of each chapter in this book, you will find an application-focused workbook section that will help you to delve deeper into the material and develop concrete steps to put these abiding principles to work for your individual and congregational needs.

In each workbook section, there will be a journal prompt. In Appendix A, you will find the STAR journaling grid, which is designed to help you discover how to journal in a meaningful way.[2] You can get a journal to accompany this book or use whatever works best for you.

I want you to understand that journaling is another form of communication with God and can become a lifestyle if you feel connected to God through His Word. This connection happens when you read His Word and apply it to your life and circumstances.

As we move forward in this book, it is important that you understand that the process will require you to learn to "self-feed" on God's Word. In using the journal, you will experience a process that will help you to become a self-feeder, and this process will likely continue for the rest of your life. I understand that many people initially feel a little intimidated by journaling until they come to see that it is not as hard or as complicated as they feared it would be.

The Swoosh

Years ago, in prayer, I had a vision of a day when I

would author many books that would help to spread the gospel of Christ to the nations. In that vision, I saw what I could only describe as a smeared fingerprint. I knew immediately what it meant.

In the environment in which I grew up, we took the biblical model of anointing with oil seriously. If you have ever taken some oil on your finger and applied it to a doorpost, to someone's forehead, or to a sheet of paper, you know the smeared fingerprint that is left behind. In this vision, I had the understanding that I wanted to anoint each copy of my books, which would leave that smeared look. I wrote this in my journal and left it there.

Years later, as I began to see the dreams of authoring Christ-centered books come to pass, I was reminded of this. Although I cannot personally anoint every book, I decided to use what I call a swoosh to designate that each book has been prayed over. My prayer is that the words in the books published will be anointed by God, bring life transformation to all who read them, and bring glory to God.

About The Abiding Network

The vision of The Abiding Network, of which I am the founder and directional leader, is to assist leaders in creating environments of discipleship to encourage followers to know Christ and make Him known. The Abiding Network was launched out of Catalyst Church in Bentonville, Arkansas, in 2013. It is a support network to help church leaders who are active in ministry know Christ and make Him known in their areas of influence.

Our heart is to network individuals, churches, non-profits, and other groups to support their kingdom calling. We offer a system of biblical accountability, encouragement, relationship building, and resource sharing to assist in their health and long-term success.

As a network, we have partnered with dozens of churches in many diverse areas. Our website (www.abidingnetwork.com) lists some of the organizations and ministries with which we have partnered for kingdom fruit. As our network grows, we add ministries to our platform so that the network expands as God leads.

The intent of Abiding Network members should be to unite in the common vision to know Christ and make Him known. We desire a unity of the Spirit that celebrates what God is doing in our world today.

Coaching

Many leaders in the business and church worlds need an outside voice for encouragement, accountability, leadership development, and organizational strategy. One aspect of The Abiding Network is to serve leaders in such a capacity—for instance, in seasons of building, transition, growth, relationship development, tragedy, and celebration. Some of the most fruitful seasons of our lives can be birthed out of a mentor or coach helping us in our journey.

We are also developing many leadership resources that are available to help church leaders navigate the short- and long-term direction and vision for their spheres of influence. I personally have been coached, and I coach many other leaders in many different ministry and secular environments.

I have found coaching to be one of the greatest catalysts for my personal and professional growth and leadership development. Sometimes we simply need a coach, like Paul was to Timothy, to help us grow into all that God intends for us.

Resources

For more information about The Abiding Network, please visit www.abidingnetwork.com. Media resources can be found at www.abidingnetwork.com/Media.

Please see Appendix B of this book for information about the Journey program and the Influencers ministry as well as a list of relevant resources, including my books *The Abiding Church*, *Abiding at the Feet of Jesus*, and *Abiding in Identity*, also published by Sermon To Book.

Introduction Questions

Question: What are some questions you have about your new-found life in Christ? Jot these down. This list will prove valuable to you as you continue to grow and mature in your walk with Christ.

_____

_____

_____

_____

_____

_____

_____

_____

_____

_____

_____

Action: Read Appendix A and become familiar with the STAR process for journaling. Acquire a journal or notebook to use for the exercises in this book and your continued study afterwards.

Journal: In your journal, write down your testimony, your story of when and how you came to know Christ. Where and when did this happen? What emotions did you feel? Whom did God use in helping you to understand the gospel? How did you change? Ask God for an opportunity to share your story with a Christian who needs to be encouraged or an unbeliever who is ready to hear how God has worked in your life.

Introduction Notes

_____

_____

_____

_____

_____

_____

_____

_____

_____

_____

_____

_____

_____

_____

_____

_____

_____

_____

_____

_____

CHAPTER ONE

Abide in Christ

I've met many Christians who hold God at arm's length, afraid to let Him get too close. They attend church, read their Bibles, and pray when something important comes up. Either they have a skewed vision of who God is, which makes them afraid of Him, or they are sure that God will make uncomfortable demands on their lives. Either way, they are distant and not abiding in Him.

To abide means to continue to remain connected. In Luke 10, Jesus was abiding at the home of Lazarus, Martha, and Mary. While Martha clattered around in the kitchen, Mary sat down at Jesus' feet and soaked up all that He was saying (Luke 10:39–40). Mary wanted to be completely connected with Christ while she was in His presence. What better place to remain connected to Christ than sitting at His feet and learning from Him as He articulates the foundations of His kingdom and the specific purpose He has for you?

John 15 paints a beautiful picture of a life that is connected to the vine of Christ. As you read, think of how this passage connects to our relationship and growth in Christ:

I am the true vine, and My Father is the vinedresser. Every branch in Me that does not bear fruit He takes away; and every branch that bears fruit He prunes, that it may bear more fruit. You are already clean because of the word which I have spoken to you. Abide in Me, and I in you. As the branch cannot bear fruit of itself, unless it abides in the vine, neither can you, unless you abide in Me.

I am the vine, you are the branches. He who abides in Me, and I in him, bears much fruit; for without Me you can do nothing. If anyone does not abide in Me, he is cast out as a branch and is withered; and they gather them and throw them into the fire, and they are burned. If you abide in Me, and My words abide in you, you will ask what you desire, and it shall be done for you. By this My Father is glorified, that you bear much fruit; so you will be My disciples.

As the Father loved Me, I also have loved you; abide in My love. If you keep My commandments, you will abide in My love, just as I have kept My Father's commandments and abide in His love.

These things I have spoken to you, that My joy may remain in you, and that your joy may be full. This is My commandment, that you love one another as I have loved you. Greater love has no one than this, than to lay down one's life for his friends. You are My friends if you do whatever I command you. No longer do I call you servants, for a servant does not know what his master is doing; but I have called you friends, for all things that I heard from My Father I have made known to you. You did not choose Me, but I chose you and appointed you that you should go and bear fruit, and that your fruit should remain, that whatever you ask the Father in My name He may give you. These things I command you, that you love one another.
—John 15:1–17

The following are some key thoughts about John 15:1–17 that you may have noticed:

- This passage emphasizes the intimacy between Christ and the Father, as well as the intimacy Christ wants with us, just like He has with the Father.

- Christ spoke about the importance of bearing fruit and the consequences for those who do not bear fruit. Did you see how the Father is glorified when we bear kingdom fruit?

- We must depend totally on Christ. Our prayer life changes when we abide in Him and have His heart.

- Notice the importance of love in this passage and how walking in His love is connected to obeying His commands and loving others.

This life produces kingdom fruit that remains in the realm of eternity. I love that we can have an intimate, abiding fellowship with God through Christ. Though we may think that abiding in Christ is difficult, the privilege of abiding in Christ is as simple as talking with our best friend.

The Simplicity of Abiding

Jesus desires to be Lord of your life and for you to exist and remain in Him. Jesus does not want you to put Him at the top of your list of things to do for the day. He does not want you to check off your time with Him like you would check off items on a grocery list or a list of household chores. Jesus wants to be the center of your life. He wants everything else in your life to flow through your relationship with Him. This is totally different from just being part of a to-do list.

The model that Christ gave us for how to be followers

is so simple that it confounds the wise of this world. Jesus told us simply to remain connected to Him. That's it. You don't need a ten-step program or a chart of accomplishments. Just stay connected to Him. Abide in Him.

What does it look like when you are abiding with Christ?

- You develop a hunger for God's Word and spend time really digging into the Bible, reflecting on what is being said and applying it to your life.

- Throughout your day, you assume a posture that allows you to hear what the Holy Spirit is saying.

- You don't look at what people will do for you; rather, you seek out ways to show God's love to others.

- Throughout the day, you find your heart seeking to draw closer to Jesus no matter what is going on around you.

- You see godly fruit all around you, not because of your efforts, but because you are in tune with what the Holy Spirit is doing in and through you.

If you were to view your spouse or friend as only a checkmark on your list, the relationship would not last for long. Your relationship with Jesus is no different. Outside of abiding in Christ, you will have an uncultivated soul overgrown with briars, thistles, and thorns.

Jesus kept things very simple and spoke practically to people. So many times, the simplicity of Christ's method is overlooked as being "too easy." People think that there must be more to it than this. "Give me something to do, and I'll do it." "Give me a ten-step program that feeds my ego, and I'll be sure to complete it." Do not lose fellowship with Him in your effort to know about Him.

As you spend time in the church and around the church world, you will notice a tendency to complicate things. Many Christians fall into the trap of thinking that the more they do, the better they are. Many will try to convince you that you need "Christ and...." They will try to add things on top of Christ for your salvation and righteousness. Many of these people are good-hearted, but they can lead you astray from abiding. Church leaders are usually the guiltiest in this area.

My ministry in life is to help people get as close to Christ as possible and to encourage them to stay there because cultivating an abiding relationship with Him results in a fruitful life. I push new believers toward proximity with Christ because proximity is the only place where abiding can begin and continue. I know that I am fruitful when Christ is formed in others and they are ready to take their abiding relationship and share it with other people. There is no greater feeling in the world than seeing people experience Christ in this way.

In moving forward, the most important thing is that you're abiding in Him. This abiding should never be overlooked in your pursuit of knowledge about God. There is a significant difference between the two, and it is easy to fall into this trap.

And we have known and believed the love that God has for us. God is love, and he who abides in love abides in God, and God in him.

—1 John 4:16

Ask God to teach you how to abide in Him. Ask Him to reveal to you the fellowship and love that is spoken of in John 15. Ask Him to show you areas in your life that need to be cut off and removed, as well as other areas that need to be pruned, so fruit can grow. Give God permission to discipline and prune you in ways that will make you grow more. As you abide and grow in Christ, you will become a better disciple for Christ and will encourage others along the way.

WORKBOOK

Chapter One Questions

Question: Would you describe your relationship with Christ as distant or connected? What fears or distractions create distance for you? What truths or steps of obedience can help you to build connection?

_____

_____

_____

_____

_____

_____

_____

_____

_____

_____

_____

_____

Question: Is your Christian walk more about *doing* or *being*? How is bearing fruit a natural result of abiding? What are the consequences of focusing one's attention on doing works for God instead of building a relationship?

_____

_____

_____

_____

_____

_____

_____

_____

_____

_____

Action: List some characteristics of a relationship that is completely dependent, such as a young child depending on his or her parents. How do these characteristics exemplify what it is like to depend on Christ? How is depending a key component of abiding?

_____

_____

_____

_____

_____

_____

_____

_____

_____

_____

_____

_____

_____

Journal: Meditate on John 15:1–17 and follow the STAR journal process. What does it mean to abide in Christ?

Chapter One Notes

_____

_____

_____

_____

_____

_____

_____

_____

_____

_____

_____

_____

_____

_____

_____

_____

_____

_____

_____

_____

_____

_____

_____

CHAPTER TWO

What Is a Disciple?

*And Jesus came and spoke to them, saying, "All authority has been given to Me in heaven and on earth. Go therefore and **make disciples** of all the nations, baptizing them in the name of the Father and of the Son and of the Holy Spirit, teaching them to observe all things that I have commanded you; and lo, I am with you always, even to the end of the age." Amen.*
                              —Matthew 28:18–20 *(emphasis added)*

If I ask, "What is a dog?" we will have similar answers. Even if we describe different breeds or various characteristics, we will agree on the attributes common to all dogs. However, if I ask people to define *disciple*, I am certain, based on my personal experience in the American church, that I will get many different answers.

What is a disciple? A true abiding church will produce fully devoted followers of Christ; that is, it will produce disciples. Let's be clear on what the word *disciple* means and what it does not.

Many people receive all their theological instruction from books or from various instructors who, in some cases, have never opened a Bible. Some folks would say that disciples are produced through a program or process that their local church has put in place. They are told that if they go through the classes offered, at the end there will be a certificate that says they are disciples. Other churches simply offer up the generic thought that any person who professes faith in Christ is a disciple. Which is correct?

I think that we need to ask ourselves sincerely, "What is a true, biblical disciple? What was Jesus' example of a disciple? What was in the DNA of a first-century disciple?" If we don't have a clear understanding of what a disciple of Christ actually is, then how can we make disciples as described in Matthew 28:18–20? If we don't know what we're moving toward, then we have no clear measure of whether or not we are being true to our Master's command.

According to Bible.org, a disciple can be defined as a learner, a pupil, an imitator, a follower, and a reproducer.[3] In Jesus' ministry, I notice a pattern that looks something like this:

- A call to come and see (Psalm 66:5; John 1:39–41)

- A call to a greater commitment (Matthew 22:37–38; Luke 14:25–33)

- A call to die to self (Matthew 16:24–26; John 15:13)

Matthew 4:19 says, "Then He said to them, 'Follow Me, and I will make you fishers of men.'" Jesus used this pattern in the initial call of the disciples, as well as in the remainder of His earthly ministry to introduce the gospel.

True Discipleship

One of the areas in which Jesus was the most dynamic was His ability to grab a person at the core of his or her being. Christ looked past the outward mask that people presented and convicted their hearts.

When Christ gets ahold of you at the deepest level, you have a decision to make: to follow Him or to reject Him. Getting a new Christian to adhere outwardly to a book of principles is not going to produce kingdom fruit, nor will it make a disciple. Kingdom fruit is produced by leading people to abide in Christ.

Jesus made this chilling accusation:

> *Woe to you, scribes and Pharisees, hypocrites! For you travel land and sea to win one proselyte, and when he is won, you make him twice as much a son of hell as yourselves.*
>
> **—Matthew 23:15**

Jesus accused the religious leaders of His day of creating followers who looked like them but were not pleasing to God. The pupils were worse off than the scribes and Pharisees themselves. Much like the teachers, the pupils worked within a system that looked religious and godly on the outside but was missing key elements.

This duplication happens in a lot of seminaries, Christian colleges, and churches in America. People go there in hopes of becoming disciples, and they come out less like Christ than when they began. In turn, they take this methodology wherever they go, and the cycle continues.

Christ does not want converts; He wants disciples. By definition, to *convert* is to "turn to another or a particular use or purpose."[4] If you can be converted to Christianity, then you can be converted to something else. Conversion does not produce long-term fruit in the life of a person. Only transformation does. (We will see more on this in chapter 6.)

Many converts are educated into a system of religion. They know what the Word says, but it stops there. Having belief in Christ or knowledge of the Bible alone is not enough to be a disciple of Christ: "You believe that there is one God. You do well. Even the demons believe—and tremble!" (James 2:19).

I have read of university-trained historians who know more Bible facts than the average Christ follower, yet they live as atheists. They put biblical knowledge on the same level as all other historical knowledge. The Scriptures are just another book of writings to them.

Education alone never produces a disciple. Education can produce a convert who buys into the system that is taught. This convert can be trained or educated toward something else later. If this person is never transformed at a heart level, then he or she is simply conforming to some new way of thinking.

Self-help books in the church sell like hotcakes because people are looking for answers to the problems they thought would be fixed when they found Christ. Most Christians love a good five-step program or a ten-step self-help book. It helps them to feel like they are in charge when they align their behavior with a certain system. What is the problem with this? Following a self-help system is not the personal and utter abandonment Christ asks of His true disciples.

Most of the time, we end up self-righteously proud of our accomplishments or unrighteously condemned for our failures. Disciples are not in control. They relinquish their control to Christ when they say, "I will follow You."

Programs do not make disciples. I want to be clear that I believe programs do have a part to play in the local church. Programs can help a believer to grow, mature, and learn. However, they don't guarantee the production of healthy, growing disciples. Jesus' model was all about proximity to Him.

It is time the church learns how to move converts to Christians, sinners to saints, and believers to disciples. We must exchange our long-distance relationships with God for close, loving relationships involving daily contact with Jesus. I think that education is important, but many times we educate our minds at the expense of our hearts, which, according to God, is backward.

Educating Our Hearts

Discipleship comes out of an intimate, abiding relationship with Christ, no other way. A renewed mind is part of the sanctification process that comes after transformation (Romans 12:2). The heart must be addressed first.

More than words on a page, discipleship is about discovery. A disciple allows God to author his or her faith and, through abiding in Christ, gives Him permission to be the finisher of that faith (Hebrews 12:2).

The first act of a believer who desires discipleship is permission. You must give Christ permission to be your Lord and submit your will to Him. Many believers in Christ are not disciples. They have fed their human tendencies with "step programs" that can accomplish what they think is good, or they have asked Jesus to be their Savior from sin, problems, sickness, and anything else that gets in the way of their best life. Jesus wants to be our Savior and our Lord.

The abiding church gives people the secret to living in God's will for the rest of their lives. First, we draw near to Jesus on a regular basis, which allows us to know what He wants to happen in our lives. Next, we follow Him in loving obedience and see His glory proclaimed in the earth. I have to tell you that it's never a formula but, rather, fellowship that gives you what you need at each moment. Fellowship transforms into a deep trust so we can come to Him in prayer.

This reminds me of the portion of the Lord's Prayer that says, "Give us this day our daily bread" (Matthew 6:11). God gave the Israelites daily manna in the desert (Exodus 16). If they tried to save some for a rainy day, then it would spoil. Trusting that God will provide each day requires faith, which pleases God. God wants us to come to Him daily for our sustenance and feeding. He wants us to abide *and remain* in Him.

Often throughout the Gospels, Jesus called people to "come and see" (John 1:39). He called them to discipleship. Jesus understood that for fruit to remain, He had to teach His followers how to abide in Him (John 15:5).

For example, Paul's pattern of ministry was to go to a place and then preach the gospel. He did not change things up every week in order to attract more people. His message was simple and clear. In the epistles, we see him address church topics and answer many questions asked of him by the churches. However, his main message was the gospel: get close to Christ and allow Him to transform you through repentance. This simplicity produced power as people connected to it and allowed it to change their lives. Paul used a similar message everywhere he went.

Discipleship is not about arriving, but about abiding in Christ. It's not about getting somewhere, but about experiencing the person of Jesus wherever He leads. If you remember, Jesus did not choose hundreds of people to continue His legacy. At the end of three years, He only had a small group of followers who carried the term *disciple* (Acts 1:15). This ragtag bunch served as the catalyst that turned this world upside down with the gospel message.

A disciple of Christ has all of the following attributes, which we will explore in the next few chapters:

- Has made Christ Lord of his or her life and has taken up his or her cross

- Has personal abandonment and absolute trust in Jesus

- Lives in a daily posture of repentance

- Is in an abiding relationship with Jesus

- Is feeding on the Word of God

- Is a reproducer of what he or she has become in Christ

How long does this take? I believe, based on Christ's model, that a person becomes a disciple the moment he or she takes up his or her cross to follow Him (Matthew 16:24). Did you know that Jesus said "if" when He called people to discipleship? "If" is the determining factor as to what will happen next. "If you forsake all else, take up your cross, and follow Me, then you are My disciple." Most people will not take this step.

Some will take this step the moment they experience God and will begin their discipleship journey. Others will call on Christ for salvation and years later will come to the place of taking up their cross to follow Him. In my opinion, a disciple is born when a believer's attitude to Jesus moves from Savior to Lord.

For many are called, but few are chosen.
—Matthew 22:14

Many believers have every intention of becoming disciples of Christ. They make lofty plans to make that commitment—at some point in the near future. Like the verse above says, we see that many are called and invited to discipleship, but few choose to come.

What you do for Jesus means nothing unless you are abiding in Him. Abiding is about fellowship with Christ and getting to know Him. I encourage you to contemplate this chapter to ensure that you have a grasp on what a biblical disciple looks like.

WORKBOOK

Chapter Two Questions

Question: How would you define *disciple*? Do you see evidence of discipleship in the lives of most professing believers? Why or why not? Would you describe yourself as a disciple?

_____

_____

_____

_____

_____

_____

_____

_____

_____

_____

_____

Question: What are some hot topics in Christian living or self-help books right now? How could each of these issues be resolved with the heart transformation that comes through discipleship? What are some possible dangers of reducing every issue to a formulaic or psychology-based solution? Have you ever depended more on a program than on Christ?

_____

_____

_____

_____

_____

_____

_____

_____

_____

_____

_____

_____

Action: *It's never a formula but, rather, fellowship that gives you what you need at each moment.* What are some formulas that Christians use to manage their lives, such as formulas that supposedly guarantee success in dating, marriage, parenting, career, ministry, or money management? What is the difference between a principle and a formula? How can you be guided by wise principles without being bound by manmade formulas? Read a biography or memoir of a Christian who exemplified discipleship. I recommend the following works: *Forged for a Vision* by Rocky Fleming, *Master Plan of Evangelism* by Billy Graham, *The Cost of Discipleship* by Dietrich Bonhoeffer, and *Mere Christianity* by C.S. Lewis. As you read, ask yourself how this person's fellowship with Christ informed his decisions, even some that were considered radical by other believers.

_____

_____

_____

_____

_____

_____

_____

_____

_____

_____

_____

_____

Journal: Study Christ's call to discipleship in Matthew 16:24 and Luke 9:23 (the verses before and after will provide helpful context as well). Follow the STAR journal process. What insight do those verses provide about fellowship over formulas in living as a disciple?

Chapter Two Notes

_____

_____

_____

_____

_____

_____

_____

_____

_____

_____

_____

_____

_____

_____

_____

_____

_____

_____

_____

_____

_____

_____

CHAPTER THREE

Self-Feeding on God's Word

Then Jesus said to those Jews who believed Him, "If you abide in My word, you are My disciples indeed."
—John 8:31

The Christian faith teaches that Jesus is the Word of God (John 1:1). He manifested in the flesh to reveal the heart of the Father to mankind. When you cultivate a hunger for God's Word and learn to self-feed on it, you are abiding in Him. This is a huge part of an intimate, abiding relationship with Christ. He speaks to us through His Word.

Cultivating a healthy diet of God's Word is a vital part of a disciple's life. Too many churches create environments where you can only be "fed the Word" when you are hearing a preacher preach in a church gathering. This could not be further from the truth.

I love the corporate gatherings in which the Bible calls us to participate. I love God-anointed teachers and preachers who help me to grow in my faith. However, God did not call us to be spoon-fed all of our lives by gifted teachers and preachers. He desires for each of us to learn to feed ourselves and live on a healthy diet of God's Word. I hope that makes sense.

> *Therefore, laying aside all malice, all deceit, hypocrisy, envy, and all evil speaking, as newborn babes, desire the pure milk of the word, that you may grow thereby, if indeed you have tasted that the Lord is gracious.*
> **—1 Peter 2:1–3**

Early in your walk with Christ, you will need a lot of spoon-feeding and teaching. A physical newborn needs milk and not meat, needs others to feed him or her, and grows in this process. We have similar needs in our spiritual journeys. As you develop and mature spiritually, you should move from milk of the Word to meat to sustain your growth:

> *For though by this time you ought to be teachers, you need someone to teach you again the first principles of the oracles of God; and you have come to need milk and not solid food. For everyone who partakes only of milk is unskilled in the word of righteousness, for he is a babe. But solid food belongs to those who are of full age, that is, those who by reason of use have their senses exercised to discern both good and evil.*
> **—Hebrews 5:12–14**

> *And I, brethren, could not speak to you as to spiritual people but as to carnal, as to babes in Christ. I fed you with milk and not with solid food; for until now you were not able to receive it, and even now you are still not able; for you are still carnal.*
> **—1 Corinthians 3:1–3a**

As we grow in our spiritual life and walk with Christ

through reading the Bible, we move away from being spoon-fed to abiding in Christ as He reveals truths to us. Reading the Bible is one of the most important things a Christ follower can do for many reasons, some of which we will explore in this book. There are so many benefits to making this a lifestyle.

The first step is to acknowledge that the Bible is God's inspired Word. He used men to pen the physical words as they were moved by the Holy Spirit. The Bible should be accepted by every believer as our infallible guide in matters pertaining to conduct and doctrine:

> *All Scripture is given by inspiration of God, and is profitable for doctrine, for reproof, for correction, for instruction in righteousness, that the man of God may be complete, thoroughly equipped for every good work.*
> *—2 Timothy 3:16–17*

The Bible is comprised of the words of eternal life: "But Simon Peter answered Him, 'Lord, to whom shall we go? You have the words of eternal life'" (John 6:68). We need to realize that these eternal words are not like a typical teaching. God's words carry weight and, when followed, have the power of redemption and freedom. Surprisingly, they also teach us the difference between theology and doctrine.

Theology Versus Doctrine

In order to lay a foundation that allows you to read further with clear perspective, you need to understand from the beginning that there is a slight difference between theology and doctrine.

Do you know the truth? Can you tell the difference between a clear, biblical doctrine and some preacher's soapbox statements? If asked, could you defend the faith you are counting on for your eternal security? Deception is very difficult to see if you are not grounded in the truth. There are many counterfeits in the world. I want you to have the truth of God so you can live it out and see fruit in your life.

> *But sanctify the Lord God in your hearts, and always be ready to give a defense to everyone who asks you a reason for the hope that is in you, with meekness and fear....*
> *—1 Peter 3:15*

The word translated "defense" is the Greek word *apologia*, which means "to give a speech in defense, vindication, defense, speak a defense." This can be a convicting thing to read if you have never been challenged in this area. I believe that a healthy church not only has clearly defined doctrine and theology, but also trains disciples to know and skillfully defend their faith.

Truth never changes. Truth does not wait for you to align with it before becoming truth. Truth always was, is, and will always be. Many people come around to truth, and others reject it. Truth does not become truth when someone believes it. Belief in truth can take effect in someone's life when he or she applies it, but it was always truth. Circumstances don't define truth; truth simply is. We want to lay a foundation that the God of the Bible is truth; therefore, we look to Him to define truth.

Today many believe that your beliefs, feelings, and experiences should define "your truth." This has gone so far that many even deny scientific facts and replace them with their feelings. It's mind-numbing how much it is happening! People subscribe to the lie that truth is relevant to each person's situation and feelings. If this is the case, there are no moral or scientific absolutes because feelings and circumstances change constantly. This is *not* a biblical understanding of truth.

If your belief changes based on circumstances, then it cannot be founded in God's words. Your belief was determined only by a temporary, changing foundation. Many Christians today do not have strong, doctrinal beliefs anchored in the rock of Christ. Instead, they have chosen to put their faith in shifting, circumstantial truths. When the circumstance or their experience changes, so does their doctrine. This should not be so in the body of Christ.

Your belief, or lack thereof, does not change the truth of God's Word. Your belief or denial simply determines if the truth will be accepted by you and allowed to benefit you or if the truth will be the very thing that condemns you. Truth is truth. It's like the law of gravity. If an atheist and a Christian both walk off of a cliff, they both will immediately experience the power of gravity. If they chose not to believe that law and, therefore, assumed that it would not affect them, they were wrong. Simply put, the law or truth does not change based on their belief or lack of belief. Their belief about the law of gravity simply allows them to benefit from it or suffer the consequences.

What Is Doctrine?

Didaskalia (did-as-kal-EE-ah): Teaching, instruction, learning or authority.[5]

When I talk about biblical doctrine, I am referring to the governing authority and supremacy of the Word of God that presides over the church body. As a disciple of Christ, you must submit to the teachings of Christ, who authored and affirmed the Scriptures. This is why doctrine is so important!

One of the key characteristics of disciples of Christ is

the high regard they place on His Word. Jesus, Peter, Paul, and others in the Scripture always pointed back to the words that they spoke as God directed. These are words that God breathed, not their own thoughts, ideas, or theology.

When the priests and Pharisees questioned Jesus about His doctrine, they often were not asking about specifics, because He always pointed back to the written Word. They were questioning Him about what authority He spoke by and essentially asking, "Who put *you* in charge?"

In the beginning was the Word, and the Word was with God, and the Word was God. He was in the beginning with God.

—John 1:1–2

But you must continue in the things which you have learned and been assured of, knowing from whom you have learned them, and that from childhood you have known the Holy Scriptures, which are able to make you wise for salvation through faith which is in Christ Jesus.

All Scripture is given by inspiration of God, and is profitable for doctrine, for reproof, for correction, for instruction in righteousness, that the man of God may be complete, thoroughly equipped for every good work.

I charge you therefore before God and the Lord Jesus Christ, who will judge the living and the dead at His appearing and His kingdom: Preach the word! Be ready in season and out of season. Convince, rebuke, exhort, with all longsuffering and teaching. For the time will come when they will not endure sound doctrine, but according to their own desires, because they have itching ears, they will heap up for themselves teachers; and they will turn their ears away from the truth, and be turned aside to fables. But you

be watchful in all things, endure afflictions, do the work of an evangelist, fulfill your ministry.
—2 Timothy 3:14–4:5

Your doctrine should be clear, firm, and unwavering. As a disciple of Christ, you should not bend on your doctrinal beliefs. The Bible is your Word from God, and it will not change. It is good, however, to understand that doctrine is to be lived out in relationship. You don't want doctrine to become dry and distant. You want to grow in and live out the doctrine of the Scriptures in intimate fellowship with Christ.

That means there is a progressive transformation process in each person's life. As you grow in your understanding and application of doctrine in the context of being part of an accountable biblical community, doctrine comes alive. That is why being connected to a strong, doctrinally based biblical community is so necessary for long-term spiritual growth.

What Is Theology?

Many people confuse and intermingle the words theology and doctrine, but they are very different:

Not that we are sufficient of ourselves to think of anything as being from ourselves, but our sufficiency is from God, who also made us sufficient as ministers of the new covenant, not of the letter but of the Spirit; for the letter kills, but the Spirit gives life.
—2 Corinthians 3:5–6

The letter of the Law can be raw and distant. The new covenant has given us access to the grace of God and the empowerment of the Spirit. Doctrine that is not empowered by the presence of God is dry and can destroy. Doctrine comes alive and is lived out as we experience God and learn of Him. He reveals Himself to us in what we like to call "theology."

Theology is defined simply as the study of the nature of God and religious beliefs. This is a wonderful definition of the life of a believer as he or she grows in discipleship. Whereas doctrine is settled and does not take into account your experience, theology is all about your journey with Christ. Theology is very much the process of learning to know God and His nature. Theology should strengthen doctrine over time. God's heart for you is that you have an intimate, abiding relationship with Him that is founded in strong doctrine and is lived out in fellowship as you learn and grow in Christ. This is theology.

Primary Issues Versus Secondary Issues | Closed-Handed Issues Versus Open-Handed Issues

At my church, we use terms like primary and secondary, closed-handed and open-handed, to define doctrine versus theology. Primary, closed-handed issues are what we would describe as doctrine. Doctrine is settled, and we don't change that. Doctrine is to be accepted, learned, and digested as we grow in our walks with Christ. Secondary and open-handed issues are what we would describe as theology.

Doctrine never changes, but our personal theology develops as we mature in Christ. While circumstance, experience, and history are part of our theology and learning about God, we must be careful not to rationalize our view of God based on our circumstances. We must be careful not to try to make doctrine align with our life experiences. Experience is a huge teacher, and I believe that it is a vital part of our spiritual maturity. However, doctrine is doctrine. Doctrine should not change merely because our circumstances or experiences have changed. Doctrine should not change because of changes in culture. I have taken many people through discipleship over the years and have walked this same journey personally. It is powerful to watch people who may struggle to grasp certain doctrinal truths grow into understanding and obedience as they live in their own intimate relationship with Christ. Remember, this is a journey, not a sprint. You have the rest of your life and even eternity to be transformed into His image.

Years ago, a lady at a church I pastored was offended that we celebrated Mother's Day as a church. She was an orphan, and she had a lot of pain associated with even the mention of mothers. In talking with her, my heart broke.

Because of her pain, this woman struggled to celebrate Mother's Day. However, that didn't mean that the day shouldn't be celebrated or that it was right for her to be angry at all mothers. At the beginning, she wanted her theology of Mother's Day to be the doctrine for our church.

Through a long season of prayer, biblical counseling, and loving people pouring into her life, we were able to help her see all the spiritual mothers that God had placed in her life. She found healing and joy, and she eventually used her story to minister to people with similar histories. God used the very thing that had once caused her such pain and agony to make her a catalyst for healing and freedom in others' lives.

As you read this, you may be tempted to give up and put this book down. You may feel like you have too much sin in your life or too much baggage to draw near to Jesus. You may think that there is too much pain, and you cannot see the other side of healing. Take those goggles off. Put off all of that junk from your past—your sorrow and your pain—and give Christ an opportunity to love you.

In the pages ahead, we are going to explore how the

kingdom of heaven is wide open for you today. God can help you to find healing from your painful past experiences and to discover new, joyous ones in Him. He wants to change your perspective. He wants to challenge your theology. He wants to remove religious things, and He invites you to abide with Him.

When Faith Is Born

The Bible is the main source of food for your spirit, or what the Bible calls your inner person. Many Christians have no problem understanding that they need multiple meals a day to sustain their physical flesh, but they struggle at the idea of having to feed their spirits. Many of us feed our flesh three meals a day while leaving our spirits malnourished with one cold snack a week. This is the opposite of building our faith:

So then faith comes by hearing, and hearing by the word of God.
                                                    —Romans 10:17

If you are going to live the abundant life that Christ promised, then you must live according to His words and way of doing things. Scripture is God's will, wisdom, and direction. Begin to develop an appetite for it. Spend time allowing it to wash over your mind and heart. Before you know it, you will be walking in communion with Christ and His purpose for your life.

For this reason we also thank God without ceasing, because when you received the word of God which you heard from us, you welcomed it not as the word of men, but as it is in truth, the word of God, which also effectively works in you who believe.

—1 Thessalonians 2:13

The Bible tells us that "without faith it is impossible to please Him" (Hebrews 11:6). It took faith for you to receive salvation. Faith is an important part of the Christian's life. For your faith to be born, developed, and expressed, you must have a healthy diet of God's Word. The Word of God is the only source that will produce faith.

Part of exercising your faith is to be a doer of God's Word. For God's Word to work in your life, you must act in obedience to what He says. Reading, studying, and memorizing God's Word is fruitless if you don't do what it says: "But be doers of the word, and not hearers only, deceiving yourselves" (James 1:22).

However, too many times Christians train their minds at the expense of their hearts. Allow a moment for that to sink in. Don't allow the knowledge of God's Word to supersede living God's Word.

Hearing without action is like living in poverty while having a drawer full of checks that you never cashed. You have access to life above poverty, but you have not acted on that access. God gives you access to a flourishing life in Him if you will be a doer of His Word.

The sooner you learn to feed yourself, the faster you will grow in your fellowship with God. However, many Christians have been trained to be spoon-fed. Every time you need something, you have to go to a pastor or priest, which keeps your relationship with God dependent on another person.

God wants you to feed yourself and fellowship in the secret place with Him only. It is in the inner chamber that your experience with God will push you to grow and, ultimately, to share His love with others.

The Bible is an endless source of life and wisdom. Right when you think that you are starting to understand some things, God will reveal more of Himself to you in His Word. He opens your eyes every day to see new and fresh things as you abide in Him.

Remember that faith is a journey, not a destination. Love the Word of God. As the world changes and the morals and standards of our society change, have faith and confidence in the unchanging Word of God.

WORKBOOK

Chapter Three Questions

Question: What are some ways you have been spoon-fed God's Word since coming to Christ? How are you beginning to self-feed? What do you find exciting and what seems intimidating about learning to feed yourself from the Word?

_____

_____

_____

_____

_____

_____

_____

_____

_____

_____

_____

Question: Read a doctrinal statement. I have included the doctrines of The Abiding Network in Appendix C for your reference, but your church or denomination should have a biblically based statement of faith. Contrast this with your personal theology, your view of God. What religious trappings or particular viewpoints do you carry from your upbringing and life experiences? Where does your theology need to shift to line up with doctrinal truth?

_____

_____

_____

_____

_____

_____

_____

_____

_____

_____

_____

Action: What are some ways you can self-feed on God's Word? Learn about spiritual disciplines, such as memorization and meditation. What are some other ways to ingest the Bible, such as listening to audio recordings? What tools are available to dig deep in your study of

Scripture? Who will hold you accountable to be a doer of the Word, not just a hearer? Decide how you will incorporate various types of self-feeding into your life and begin implementing your plan this week.

_____

_____

_____

_____

_____

_____

_____

_____

_____

_____

_____

_____

Journal: Look back over the many passages about God's Word shared in this chapter. Choose one that stands out to you and meditate on it using the STAR journal process. What does it teach you about the Bible and its role in your life?

Chapter Three Notes

CHAPTER FOUR

Introduction to the Holy Spirit

This chapter is about making you aware of the Holy Spirit's role in the life of a believer and introducing you to Him. Many times, people don't know about or acknowledge this person of the Godhead. Many Christians will live their whole lives without understanding the huge importance of the Holy Spirit.

From beginning to end of the Bible, the Holy Spirit is at work on behalf of Christ and God the Father. As you grow in your fellowship with God, the Holy Spirit will be there in as much of a role as you allow. He always glorifies God and confirms the Word. He brings conviction, truth, peace, help, strength, guidance, and power for daily living. He helps us in prayer and prays on our behalf. His job description is endless. The Holy Spirit exists to help you experience God. I encourage you to look for the Holy Spirit's role in your life as you read the Word and pray.

The Person of the Holy Spirit

From Genesis to Revelation, the Holy Spirit was an active participant, yet many Christians today have no clue about Him. His credentials as God are seen in passages such as the following:

> *Then God said, "Let Us make man in Our image...."*
> —**Genesis 1:26a**

> *In the beginning God created the heavens and the earth. The earth was without form, and void; and darkness was on the face of the deep. And the Spirit of God was hovering over the face of the waters.*
> —**Genesis 1:1–2**

> *But the Spirit of the LORD came upon Gideon; then he blew the trumpet, and the Abiezrites gathered behind him.*
> —**Judges 6:34**

> *When all the people were baptized, it came to pass that Jesus also was baptized; and while He prayed, the heaven was opened. And the Holy Spirit descended in bodily form like a dove upon Him, and a voice came from heaven which said, "You are My beloved Son; in You I am well pleased."*
> —**Luke 3:21–22**

In these above passages, we see the threefold expression of God and the Holy Spirit's part as God. We also see Him addressed as a personality, not an "it." I hear people all the time addressing the Holy Spirit as an "it" or a mystical ghostly mist. He is the third person of the Godhead. He is God and should be honored accordingly.

Take the time to consider what Jesus was saying about the Holy Spirit when teaching the disciples:

And I will pray the Father, and He will give you another Helper, that He may abide with you forever—the Spirit of truth, whom the world cannot receive, because it neither sees Him nor knows Him; but you know Him, for He dwells with you and will be in you.

—John 14:16–17

The Role of the Holy Spirit

In the passage above, we see Jesus talk about the person He was going to send to be another Helper. This meant another one like Him. This person was going to come alongside believers and fulfill the role that Christ had had in their lives up until that point. This is so very important because Jesus made it clear that He was not going to leave them orphans or unprepared to fulfill the Great Commission. He was giving them everything they needed to be successful as abiding leaders.

The Greek word that is used for "helper" here is *paraklētos*. This word is translated as an intercessor, consoler, advocate, or comforter.[6] That sure sounds encouraging to me. Who would not want all the things that the word implies?

Don't you think that Jesus knew what He was doing? He was not making a mistake when He taught the disciples this. If you are going to abide in Christ and encourage others to abide in Christ, you must understand the importance of what Jesus was instituting here:

These things I have spoken to you while being present with you. But the Helper, the Holy Spirit, whom the Father will send in My name, He will teach you all things, and bring to your remembrance all things that I said to you.

—John 14:25–26

> ..."What no eye has seen, nor ear heard, nor the heart of man imagined, what God has prepared for those who love him"—these things God has revealed to us through the Spirit. For the Spirit searches everything, even the depths of God. For who knows a person's thoughts except the spirit of that person, which is in him? So also no one comprehends the thoughts of God except the Spirit of God. Now we have received not the spirit of the world, but the Spirit who is from God, that we might understand the things freely given us by God. And we impart this in words not taught by human wisdom but taught by the Spirit, interpreting spiritual truths to those who are spiritual.
> **—1 Corinthians 2:9–13** (ESV)

I love the thought here. Jesus was reminding them that there was so much more He could not cram into the brief time He was with them, but that was okay. Jesus was giving them more than an answer book. He was giving them the answer. He was giving them the key to staying connected to the vine. He was giving them the way to abide, the Holy Spirit.

In general, programs and Bible studies give you specific tools and steps for specific scenarios. This can be good, but what happens when you come up against something you never studied for? What if your training did not include the answers to your current crisis?

Jesus has given you something so much better. He has given you the answer, the Holy Spirit. An abider in Christ relies less on the operating principles and more on the empowerment of the direct voice of the Holy Spirit to lead and guide. How awesome is this?

The Holy Spirit desires to direct our path, according to His righteousness. Too many Christians write off the responsibility that God gives us to hear His voice. They claim that if something is really God's will, then He will make it happen. An abider in Christ will hear His voice and obey.

There are things God wants to reveal to you, but they have to come through spiritual discernment. We can know the mind of Christ and follow His blueprint with clarity by leaning into this relationship as a part of our abiding. What an amazing gift God has given us in the Holy Spirit! If you are not looking for this relationship, then you could pass Him by every day of your life and miss what God is wanting to reveal to you:

Likewise the Spirit also helps in our weaknesses. For we do not know what we should pray for as we ought, but the Spirit Himself makes intercession for us with groanings which cannot be uttered. Now He who searches the hearts knows what the mind of the Spirit is, because He makes intercession for the saints according to the will of God.

And we know that all things work together for good to those who love God, to those who are the called according to His purpose.

—Romans 8:26-28

These verses remind us that God has a purpose and destiny for us that will work out for our good. The Holy Spirit will help us to pray and find that out. He intercedes on our behalf and can help us to pray. Prayer is such an important part of abiding in Christ. The more you abide, the less you come to God with petitions. The more you abide, the more you come to Him simply to be in His presence and remain in Him. You learn to let Him take care of the needs and petitions that used to worry you. You understand that He promised to take care of the everyday needs, and He simply wants to abide with you.

A Powerful Prayer Life

But you shall receive power when the Holy Spirit has come upon you; and you shall be witnesses to Me in Jerusalem, and in all Judea and Samaria, and to the end of the earth.
—Acts 1:8

I am not sure about you, but I need daily power to live a successful walk with Christ. There is so much sin and depravity in our world that in my human ability, I simply don't have the tools to overcome, let alone lead others. However, Jesus made provision for that as well. The verse above is one of the last recorded statements that Jesus made. He told His followers that there was more to learn.

Behold, I send the Promise of My Father upon you; but tarry in the city of Jerusalem until you are endued with power from on high.
—Luke 24:49

Jesus was saying, "You need what I am giving, and you are going to love Him." The Greek word translated as "power" is *dunamis*. The definition is "force," "miraculous power," "ability," "abundance," "might," "power," or "strength."[7] Jesus has given us the Holy Spirit to act as a miraculous power in our lives, that we might lean on His strength to help us move forward into a new, abiding relationship with God as an empowered abider in Christ.

In addition to the *dunamis* power that Jesus promised, we see other places where the Spirit uniquely empowers us with His presence. In this book I don't have the space to go into great detail on all of the specifics, but when you get to know the person of the Holy Spirit, He expresses

Himself through you in several ways.

Below are all of the relevant Greek words, each with its definition and one of many possible Scripture references:

- *Plēroō*: to fulfill, fill, or complete (Ephesians 5:18–19)[8]

- *Charis*: (empowering) grace, favor, gift (Acts 4:33)[9]

- *Charisma*: (empowering) gift of grace, free (spiritual) gift, ability or power the Holy Spirit gives to the church (1 Corinthians 12:4)[10]

- *Chrisma*: anointing, unction, something smeared like an ointment (1 John 2:20)[11]

Throughout the New Testament and church history, we see examples of people who yielded their lives to the Holy Spirit, and signs followed them.

Are you yielding to the Holy Spirit? Have you understood and walked with Him and experienced the fruits and gifts?

WORKBOOK

Chapter Four Questions

Question: What questions or misunderstandings do you have about the person or role of the Holy Spirit? How have you experienced His working in your life? How would it make a difference if you were consistently to depend on His help and strength to be an abiding disciple of Christ?

_____

_____

_____

_____

_____

_____

_____

_____

_____

_____

Question: What does it look like for the Holy Spirit to guide you in making a decision? If you are a new believer, it may be helpful to ask more mature believers to share their experiences in listening to and obeying the Spirit's guidance, particularly in difficult situations that are not directly addressed in Scripture.

Action: What does it mean to walk in the Spirit (Romans 8), to manifest the fruit of the Spirit (Galatians 5), to quench the Spirit (1 Thessalonians 5:19), and to grieve the Spirit (Ephesians 4:30)? Study these passages and the insight they give into the believer's relationship with the Holy Spirit.

_____

_____

_____

_____

_____

_____

_____

_____

_____

_____

_____

Journal: Meditate on Christ's promise of the Holy Spirit in John 14:15–31. Follow the STAR journal process. How is having the gift of the Holy Spirit superior even to Jesus' physical presence in the world?

Chapter Four Notes

CHAPTER FIVE

Lifestyle of Repentance

If the Holy Spirit is our abiding fellowship in Christ, then the purpose of the Holy Spirit is to work in our lives, giving us direction and conviction. God placed the Holy Spirit to convict us as we strive to live like Christ.

You don't avoid sin by avoiding the pleasure of sin. You avoid it by finding the superior pleasure God intended.

—Unknown origin

From that time Jesus began to preach and to say, "Repent, for the kingdom of heaven is at hand."

—Matthew 4:17

After Jesus was baptized—and then tempted in the wilderness by Satan—He began His preaching ministry with a call to repentance: "Repent, for the kingdom of heaven is at hand" (Matthew 4:17). This is a foundational truth of Christianity that applies to all people. The first thing that has to happen for a person to be reconciled to God is the acknowledgment of his or her sin. If you cannot admit guilt as a result of your sin, then God cannot apply His grace to your life. Grace follows repentance. God can pour out His love and goodness to you every day, but until you confront your sin and acknowledge it before God, forgiveness cannot flow on your behalf. The word *repent* is defined as follows:

1. To change one's mind or purpose.[12]

2. To feel sorry ... or contrite for past conduct; regret or be conscience-stricken about a past action [or] attitude.[13]

3. To feel such sorrow for sin or fault as to be disposed to change one's life for the better.[14]

Repentance is to turn from sin to God. When you repent, it's not simply a change of mind, but such a change as would reverse the effects of the previous state of mind. Many times, people feel guilt and even remorse for the sin they have allowed in their lives. They feel bad, but not enough to make a change and head the other way. This is like a kid saying, "I'm sorry," because his mom caught him with his hand in the cookie jar. The kid is not having a true change of heart and the desire to set off in the opposite direction. He is only sorry because he got caught. If he had not gotten caught, he wouldn't have thought twice about disobeying his mother.

True repentance acknowledges sin and then makes the adjustments to stay away from committing that sin ever again. Even as a follower of Christ with a new nature, you will fall short and sin at times. Make certain to live in a posture of repentance so your heart is sensitive to honoring God's Word in obedience. Repentance should be a *daily acknowledgment* in the life of a believer. This is known as godly conviction, which produces right actions and thoughts.

What Produces Godly Conviction?

For godly sorrow produces repentance leading to salvation, not to be regretted; but the sorrow of the world produces death.

—*2 Corinthians 7:10*

The verse above demonstrates the point that worldly sorrow can work on your emotions and cause guilt for what you have done. Many people in prison today feel bad about the crimes they committed that got them there. Unfortunately, the rate of people returning to prison after time served is huge in the United States. This is because their sin was only caged and never dealt with. The minute they were no longer subdued, they fell back into the same sin. They felt sorrow for the crime, but not a godly sorrow. In the end, worldly sorrow does not lead to repentance.

If you live a lifestyle of an unrepentant heart, the scripture says that it will produce death in your life. On the other hand, if you are sensitive to the Spirit of God inside you now, He will give you a godly sorrow that will lead you to repentance.

Repentance opens the floodgates of God's grace and salvation. I pray that you get ahold of this message that Christ preached so strongly. Many churches today are not preaching repentance.

If we confess our sins, He is faithful and just to forgive us our sins and to cleanse us from all unrighteousness.
—*1 John 1:9*

Confessing and being cleansed of sin and unrighteousness is very different from condemnation and guilt. Conviction is the godly sorrow that invites us into repentance. If you are in Christ and you are feeling guilt or condemnation, that is not from God because God convicts, but Satan condemns.

When you confess your sin, you have looked it square in the eyes and acknowledged it. You are not trying to hide it from God or anyone else. You are saying that you're not just sorry because you got caught; your heart is broken because you sinned against God. God's Word says that when we do this, God "is faithful and just to forgive us our sins and to cleanse us from all unrighteousness" (1 John 1:9). What a great promise we have been given! God will forgive you every time.

Reasons People Don't Repent

1. Ignorance. Some people are simply unaware of their sin. Many non-believers do not know that they need to be reconciled to God. They go about their daily lives, living for themselves, empty and lacking eternal fulfillment.

2. Pride. Many people are so full of pride and ego that they don't see their need for God or repentance. They feel that they have done well all these years without Him, so why should they give up anything for Him?

3. Deception. Others are deceived by Satan into thinking that things are good just the way they are. Some people are in false religions that offer hope in a way other than Christ. They are deceived into thinking that faith in their god or gods is good enough to get them to bliss in the afterlife.

4. The love of sin. Still others love the lifestyle of sin that they are living. They do not want to give up the passing pleasure of sin for what they perceive about God. They do not understand that the sin in which they are living is a counterfeit of God.

These four points are why it is so important for us to follow in Jesus' steps, preach this message, and make Him known to the world. People need to hear the good news of what repentance offers them. We must share the love of Christ and give people a chance to experience God for themselves so that they, too, might uncover the beauty of abiding in Christ.

When you are in an intimate, abiding relationship with Christ and you fall short, you should feel empowered to run to Him and not from Him. If you are insecure about your relationship with God or have an unhealthy understanding of God, you will run from Him rather than to Him. When you sin, do you think to yourself, "God is going to be mad, so I need to stay away from Him for now," or do you say, "I have sinned against my loving Father. I must go to Him to restore the fellowship we have"? One response shows a healthy, abiding relationship, and the other shows an unhealthy relationship. I want you to have confidence in your fellowship with God and find joy in repentance. (You can read more about this in my book *Abiding in Identity*.)

Baptism, the Posture of Repentance

I want to close this chapter by introducing you to the church ordinance of baptism. Though it might seem strange to introduce baptism in a chapter on repentance, baptism is essentially a public confession that you will live in a posture of repentance. Many times in Scripture, we see baptism associated with repentance. As you begin to read your Bible, take note of how often the two are mentioned together. For example:

Repent therefore and be converted, that your sins may be

blotted out, so that times of refreshing may come from the presence of the Lord.

—Acts 3:19

Then Peter said to them, "Repent, and let every one of you be baptized in the name of Jesus Christ for the remission of sins; and you shall receive the gift of the Holy Spirit."

—Act 2:38

Baptism in water is by immersion, is a direct commandment of our Lord, and is for believers only. The ordinance is a symbol of the Christian's identification with Christ in His death, burial, and resurrection. I encourage you to sit with the pastor at the church where you are planted and have him share in more detail about this topic.

If we adopt a lifestyle of healthy repentance, keeping short accounts with God, we will be brought closer to the Lord because we are continually abiding in Him.

WORKBOOK

Chapter Five Questions

Question: In what ways do you find it difficult to be honest about your sin and genuinely turn from it? When you sin, do you tend to run *to* God or *from* Him? How can you make repentance a lifestyle?

_____

_____

_____

_____

_____

_____

_____

_____

_____

_____

_____

Question: Describe a time when you were in each of these situations: ignorant of your sin, filled with pride and unwilling to admit your need to repent, deceived about the state of your soul, or in love with your sin and clinging to it. How could you encourage others in these various situations to understand the blessings of repentance?

_____

_____

_____

_____

_____

_____

_____

_____

_____

_____

_____

Action: Study the two ordinances of the church, baptism and communion. How does each relate to repentance (Acts 2:38 and 1 Corinthians 11:27–32)? Talk to your pastor about how your church observes baptism and communion. If you have not been part of both of these since trusting Christ as your Savior, make plans to be baptized by immersion and to partake of the Lord's Table.

Journal: Read Psalm 139 and take time to meditate on God's amazing, intimate knowledge of you and everlasting love for you. Use the STAR journal process to focus on verses 23–24, asking God to reveal any sin in your life of which you need to repent.

Chapter Five Notes

CHAPTER SIX

Transformation Versus Conformation

In looking at our current relationship with Christ, we must evaluate whether we are transforming to Christlikeness or conforming to Christlikeness. One good way to determine this is to ask yourself whether you would be able to regulate your nature and still be a good person if all the checks and balances were removed from your life. True transformation would reveal a personal, abiding relationship in Christ if this were so. Conformation, on the other hand, is simply conforming, without necessarily making it personal.

One of the most powerful things that an intimate, abiding relationship with Christ does is to transform us. When people are in an intimate, abiding relationship with Christ, there will be transformation in their lives, and then they will see other kingdom fruit.

All biblical transformation begins with nearness to Christ. This is the Christ model. There is no program, class, or sermon series that can transform a person. Getting people close to Christ allows the opportunity for the transformation process to take place and produces disciples.

We must keep at the forefront of our passion the understanding that we all are simple vessels of God. We cannot fix or change anyone else. Let's be honest and admit that if we had the courage, we would take off our masks and reveal that we are works in progress and cannot even fix ourselves.

When it comes to discipleship, you can argue about the ways churches do things differently and whether or not those discipleship practices are healthy. However, you cannot argue with the fruit of transformed lives. Unfortunately, in all seriousness, churches often try to get people to do outward things, such as conforming to their church rules, traditions, and regulations. This is not the Christ model, and it does not produce transformed lives.

The model that Christ does offer us, however, is found in the Gospels, where He taught His disciples and then sent them out to disciple others. Equally, church leaders and believers should lovingly disciple new believers toward relationship with Christ.

Church Leadership and Discipleship

The hardest part of discipleship is walking with people on their journeys from brokenness toward wholeness because discipleship is messy, costly, and time-consuming. People travel on their individual journeys at their own pace. Learning to walk with people on this journey with grace, truth, accountability, and patience is a work of the Holy Spirit and very difficult on the soul.

The greatest joy of discipleship with people, however, is walking with them on their transformation journey of intimacy with Christ. This is what makes all the investment so rewarding. When people finally get it and they walk in their God-given blueprint, it reminds you why you do what you do. *Life transformation is the greatest measure of leading people in discipleship.* It is important that church leaders understand the parameters of their position. I have witnessed that church leaders who make the following their focus see transformed lives in their churches. When you look for a local church, consider how well church leaders do the following:

- Connect the Head to the Body

- Help people to get into proximity with Christ and, eventually, into intimate, abiding relationship with Him

- Equip the saints to do the work of the ministry

- Make disciples by helping to develop members spiritually and release them into their areas of gifting and influence—including reproduction and mentoring of spiritual fathers and mothers

Church leaders are called to equip the saints so the church can be unified. If they do their part, under Christ, His church can grow and mature, allowing each joint and member to do its own part in the body (Ephesians 4:16). Leaders are not called to do all the work themselves. They must lead people as close to Christ as allowed and then allow Him to do the work of transformation. Conforming people to a set of bylaws, membership commitments, or other church mission statements only works in conforming people, not transforming their lives.

As soon as the outward encouragement stops, people revert to the way they have always done things. Worse yet, many of these church members only hang around and participate in your church because it makes them feel good, eases their guilt, or feeds their faulty belief that they have to earn their salvation. These members do good deeds to try to be right with God rather than the good deeds being the fruit of a right standing with God through salvation. Unsurprisingly, they remain carnal, unchanged people and never seem to grow. I once met a lady who led the Sunday school program at a large church for many years until she got offended and left. When I talked with her about why she no longer was a part of that church, she said that she never bought into the "Christian thing" and only taught Sunday school because she loved kids and it made her feel good. How sad it is that she never experienced transformation in Christ but only conformed to the religious organization to fill a need in her life.

The Danger of Conformation

Many people will choose not to pursue an intimate, abiding relationship with Christ. They will simply conform outwardly without any inward transformation. A great example of this was one of Jesus' disciples, Judas. He was one of the closest to Christ while He was here on the earth, yet Judas missed the entire abiding concept. Just being around Christ does not ensure transformation. However, transformation can only happen in proximity with Christ.

When I say *conform*, I mean "to act in accordance or harmony [with something]; to comply; to act in accordance with the prevailing standards, attitudes, practices, etc., of society or a group; to be or become similar in form...."[15] When you conform to something or someone, it is often outward only. You can conform to and still never buy into the vision or practice of the organization. You are looking to get something out of it. When it comes to the church, we tend to think that if we can get the outside lined up, then the inside will be changed as well. This is not the biblical way.

Conformation is like dealing with a physical symptom without ever addressing the root cause of the problem. If the root is intact, the symptoms will never fully be healed. Years ago, I was diagnosed with psoriasis. The symptoms of this disease are many, but the main one is dry, flaky skin. My body was covered with an inflamed rash that was painful and drained the life from me. The dermatologist gave me shots and topical creams to try to heal the symptoms, but I was only getting worse.

The dirty secret about psoriasis is that there is typically a catalyst that ignites the flare-ups in your body. In my body, it was streptococcus. What the dermatologist was unaware of was that I had a tooth that was infected with streptococcus, and this was causing the psoriasis symptoms to persist.

Once I got the tooth fixed and the infection cleared up, the other symptoms went away quickly. When I addressed only the outside issue, the symptoms didn't go away. When I addressed the inside, the root issue, the outside change reflected what had happened inside.

The same is true about sin and holiness. Too many times, we tell people to stop doing this or that and focus on changing the outward symptoms while never addressing the inner issue of the sinful heart. This leaves people striving to do better without any real hope of change.

Jesus clearly understood and preached that salvation is an inward work that produces outward manifestations of that change. Conformation has to be patterned after something. To what are we conforming?

And do not be conformed to this world, but be transformed by the renewing of your mind, that you may prove what is that good and acceptable and perfect will of God.
*—**Romans 12:2***

We conform to standards of behavior in many environments, such as work, school, church, and even gyms. The danger is that some religious bodies encourage conformity to behaviors that don't align with Scripture. God does not want us to have anything between us and Him. The last place this should be happening is in the local church, yet many denominations and church networks thrive on conforming people to their own ways of doing things. Many ask for a continual outward conformation and draw people into systems, not Christ. That sounds dangerously close to getting in the way of God's glory. Billy Graham once said that he never touched the glory of God, for he knew that the moment he did, God would remove it from his life and ministry.[16]

All throughout the Bible, we see where leaders chose the less honorable thing. Many times, they settled for an idol or an image that produced nothing but problems and separation from God. They pursued an outside image and sought to conform to it.

Jeremiah struggled with this when he told the people of God:

> "Be astonished, O heavens, at this, and be horribly afraid; be very desolate," says the LORD. "For My people have committed two evils: They have forsaken Me, the fountain of living waters, and hewn themselves cisterns—broken cisterns that can hold no water."
> —*Jeremiah 2:12–13*

The people of God had exchanged God's glory for a form or image that was lifeless and worthless. Second Timothy 3:5 confirms this point of why we need to cultivate the everlasting abiding in Christ so that we guard against "having a form of godliness but denying its power."

It seems to be our natural human tendency to create systems that promote us and our agendas. I think that we are drawn to them. However, it is a deceptive tool of the enemy to keep people looking at the image or form rather than the real thing. Conforming to anything does not produce internal change. The test is in the fruit that is being produced.

Jesus told the following parable:

> *Two men went up to the temple to pray, one a Pharisee and the other a tax collector. The Pharisee stood and prayed thus with himself, "God, I thank You that I am not like other men—extortioners, unjust, adulterers, or even as this tax collector. I fast twice a week; I give tithes of all that I possess." And the tax collector, standing afar off, would not so much as raise his eyes to heaven, but beat his breast, saying, "God, be merciful to me a sinner!" I tell you, this man went down to his house justified rather than the other; for everyone who exalts himself will be humbled, and he who humbles himself will be exalted.*
> **—Luke 18:10–14**

When you address the outside of a person only, it is an attempt to modify the way he or she acts. Behavior modification works around our sin nature. It doesn't fix the problem of our hearts.

True transformation is more than mere conforming; it is soul-deep. It results in a new inner person, evidenced by outward behavior. Conformity is about the rules. Transformation is about knowing the rule-Maker.

We try to rearrange the flesh's success to rule our lives, and it produces one of two results:

The first result is pride. The Pharisee in the passage above was quick to condemn all the "other men" (Luke

18:11), especially the tax collector standing outside. He had a list of all the behaviors he did and didn't do that affirmed his righteousness. He fasted and tithed. He was a faithful attendee of the synagogue. He had to feel pretty good about himself. After all, his definition of spirituality was wrapped up in his actions. He fell in line with everyone else's expectations. Matters of the heart were not important. This produced a pride that blinded him to his true needs. He needed a transformation of the heart, as every man does.

The second result is that conforming externally will produce condemnation. We see this from both the Pharisee looking down on the tax collector and the tax collector, who was ashamed of himself. Failure and discouragement are the fruits of this kind of thinking. Condemnation from the Pharisee said that the tax collector shouldn't be allowed in the temple, and it also meant that the tax collector agreed.

When we decide that we will be saved through our own goodness, we enter a cycle I call "treadmill Christianity." Your salvation is like running on a treadmill. Every day, you are depending on your own strength and ability, running but never getting anywhere. You get tired and eventually fall off and bloody yourself up. When you have been eaten alive with self-loathing and condemnation, you get back on the treadmill in the hopes that your good works will put you back into God's good graces.

Over and over, you fail and become more discouraged until, one day, you recognize that you have had enough. You give up and quit trying. Many churches are feeding these types of behavior, while people are growing further away from Christ. Conformation never saved anyone, and it never will. In contrast, it is our perseverance in abiding in Christ that produces ultimate transformation in our lives.

The Freedom of Transformation

When we think of transformation, we don't often think that it gives us freedom, but it does. The dictionary definition of *transformation* is a "change in form, appearance, nature, or character."[17] We see this clearly displayed in Ezekiel when the Lord said:

> *I will give you a new heart and put a new spirit within you; I will take the heart of stone out of your flesh and give you a heart of flesh. I will put My Spirit within you and cause you to walk in My statutes, and you will keep My judgments and do them.*
>
> *—Ezekiel 36:26–27*

Our goal should be personal and spiritual transformation from the inside out, a process that only God is capable of working in us. Transformation is a change of our nature. One definition is the process of metamorphosis, such as when a caterpillar goes through a change inside of a cocoon. During this process, we don't see a caterpillar or a butterfly; we simply see a cocoon.

A lot happens between the time when the caterpillar enters the cocoon and when it comes out as a beautiful butterfly. Christ desires to do a work in our spirits that will produce change in our minds, wills, and emotions. He desires that we be so connected to Him that people see less of us and more of Him.

We try to address the physical and mental problems in people while Jesus goes straight to the heart, knowing that a change of the heart will produce change in the other areas. When you focus on trying to stop sinning or on making outward changes, you simply magnify the issues, and you often leave condemned.

When you are born again, your heart is changed and

made alive to Christ. The Holy Spirit does a re-creative work, and then you are different because you are a new creation. This is an immediate change that is glorious and amazing. You are empowered through the Holy Spirit for godly living, although you still have a mind, emotions, and flesh that have been trained to live according to the sin nature.

Part of the transformation process that Christ desires to do in you involves allowing His Spirit to change you from the inside out. This goes against everything you have ever known and experienced, and it is brutal. What happens, if you let it, is the death of your sinful nature, the renewal of your mind, and the dominance of your regenerated spirit. That's biblical transformation.

This process of transformation and renewal of the mind will change you incrementally into the image of God until the consummation of salvation at Christ's return. This is expressed clearly in the following verses:

Now the Lord is the Spirit; and where the Spirit of the Lord is, there is liberty. But we all, with unveiled face, beholding as in a mirror the glory of the Lord, are being transformed into the same image from glory to glory, just as by the Spirit of the Lord.
—2 Corinthians 3:17–18

What a powerful expression of transformation! God has given us complete liberty by imparting the Holy Spirit into us. He then proceeds to transform us into His image from one degree of glory to the next.

We must ensure that we are, first and foremost, submitting ourselves to be transformed. Then, as leaders, we should be focused on pointing others to Christ so He can transform them, rather than trying to change their behavior ourselves.

In a true abiding relationship with Christ, this transformation will continue and reveal more and more of God to us. At the same time, this will produce a change from our old man into Christ's likeness and image, which is essentially a renewing of the mind.

Renewing the Mind

When Christ renews our minds, it is similar to exchanging negative thoughts for positive thoughts. It involves putting off the old, sinful nature in exchange for the new, righteous nature. However, as with all transition and transformation, it is not necessarily easy.

The battle of renewing the mind is found in Romans, chapters 7 and 8. Paul described some seemingly double-minded behavior as he experienced the war that was taking place within his own being. He seemed confused and out of control:

For what I am doing, I do not understand. For what I will to do, that I do not practice; but what I hate, that I do. If, then, I do what I will not to do, I agree with the law that it is good. But now, it is no longer I who do it, but sin that dwells in me. For I know that in me (that is, in my flesh) nothing good dwells; for to will is present with me, but how to perform what is good I do not find. For the good that I will to do, I do not do; but the evil I will not to do, that I practice. Now if I do what I will not to do, it is no longer I who do it, but sin that dwells in me.
—Romans 7:15–20

At the end of chapter 7, Paul concluded that his spirit-self was alive to Christ, while his flesh-self was alive to the sin nature. He said that he would choose to "serve the law of God" with his mind (Romans 7:25b). Paul gave us a nugget of truth regarding something that is vital to a healthy walk in Christ: the renewal of our minds.

Your mind involves your thoughts and your will. The human will is the most powerful thing God created. With your will, you can choose to serve God or reject Him. Paul essentially said that the war within his mind ended when he allowed his mind to choose to serve the law of God and he put to death the body of sin.

In chapter 8, Paul expounded upon living in the spirit and having his mind renewed. He said that a carnal mind that sides with the fleshly, sinful nature is at war with God and is His direct enemy.

> *For the law of the Spirit of life in Christ Jesus has made me free from the law of sin and death. For what the law could not do in that it was weak through the flesh, God did by sending His own Son in the likeness of sinful flesh, on account of sin: He condemned sin in the flesh, that the righteous requirement of the law might be fulfilled in us who do not walk according to the flesh but according to the Spirit.*
> —**Romans 8:2-4**

This explains why we have so many religious people who have simply tried to conform to the system in place in the hierarchy of their churches. They subdue their sin nature as much as possible with fleshly disciplines and self-control. Many times, this produces extreme condemnation and eventual hopelessness, as a conformed individual will always lose the battle against his or her sin nature.

Go ahead and get back on the treadmill. You will never find peace and rest until you stop conforming and begin to allow Christ to transform you. Paul wrote:

> *I beseech you therefore, brethren, by the mercies of God,*

that you present your bodies a living sacrifice, holy, acceptable to God, which is your reasonable service. And do not be conformed to this world, but be transformed by the renewing of your mind, that you may prove what is that good and acceptable and perfect will of God.

—Romans 12:1-2

In these verses, Paul continued the thought of conformation versus transformation. He strongly encouraged us to allow our flesh to be crucified as a living sacrifice, which is the only thing we can do with the flesh. He then affirmed the transformation principle of not allowing our minds to be conformed to this world's system and way of doing things.

First John talks about the spirit of the world and the spirit of the antichrist, which is already at work in this world (1 John 2:18–22). This spirit is contrary to Christ and will produce death, not life. Many believers don't understand the significance of protecting their minds from conforming to the world's system. As abiding believers, we must allow our minds to be renewed by the Spirit of God so that we can stay connected to Christ and follow His will.

In your local church, have you noticed an environment of conforming to religious activity at the expense of a discipleship platform that promotes transformation through an intimate, abiding relationship with Christ? If so, now is the time to acknowledge it and begin to ask the Holy Spirit to help you be a catalyst within your church to make some changes or find a church that focuses on transformation, not conformation.

Transformation is slow and tough, as it takes time for people to go through this process and start to see the results on the outside. However, true and lasting fruit will come because of the inner issues that are being addressed and made right.

Most religions emphasize a requirement for us to do something to be in their gods' good graces. They have us pursuing a god and trying to be good enough. Christianity is God's story of Him pursuing us. He says, "I understand your sin and failure, and I have provided a way to be in relationship with you."

Unfortunately, many see the Christian church as another system of dos and don'ts that focuses on what we are against, rather than what we are for. Remember that the church is the hope of the world and Christ is the answer to our world's sin problem. We must examine our churches and allow this abiding principle of transformation to permeate their very DNA. You will see fruit like never before that is sustainable and reproducible. What is more compelling than eternal fruit?

People who have an intimate, abiding relationship with Jesus have been and will continue to be transformed. They understand their relationship with God and have allowed that to change their hearts. They do not pursue a lifestyle of sin because they have found the greater joy of being transformed into the image of God (Romans 8:18–19).

This transformation has removed many sinful tendencies from their hearts, and their hearts seek to honor Christ. They view their struggles with sin as opportunities to sit with Jesus and allow His power and love to conquer the sin nature.

The more time we spend with Jesus, the more we reflect His love and heart. That, my friend, is what it means to be a disciple of Christ.

WORKBOOK

Chapter Six Questions

Question: What are some areas in your life where you are aware of your need for Christ's transformation? How have external attempts to change your feelings or modify your behavior failed? Are you ready to begin the process of true and lasting change through an abiding relationship and obedient discipleship? Why or why not?

_____

_____

_____

_____

_____

_____

_____

_____

Question: Is your church focused on conforming its members to a particular system? If so, how and to what? Or does your church provide a platform for discipleship? If this is the case, are you allowing yourself to be discipled? In your church, do you see the warning signs of pride and/or condemnation, or do you observe the fruit of freedom and changed hearts that comes from true transformation? If your church is focused on conformation only, ask the Holy Spirit for wisdom to know if you can become a catalyst for change or if you need to find a different fellowship that will help you to live an abiding life.

_____

_____

_____

_____

_____

_____

_____

_____

_____

_____

_____

Action: Systems to make people conform from the outside are often called "legalism." In New Testament times, many gentile Christians were told that they had to keep the Jewish law to be right with God. Read Paul's response to legalism in the book of Galatians. What are some systems of legalism at work in churches (and in cults or false religions) today? What does the book of Galatians teach about transformation?

_____

_____

_____

_____

_____

_____

_____

_____

_____

_____

_____

Journal: Use the STAR journal process to meditate on Romans 12:1–2. Commit to transformation and ask God to teach you how to renew your mind in His truth.

Chapter Six Notes

CHAPTER SEVEN

Help on Your Journey

God did not design us to do life alone. He called us to live in biblical community with others to help us along our journeys in Christ. I like to say that I believe God created us deficient by design when we try to do life alone. Part of our DNA is to be in healthy, biblical community.

When you get around the American church, sometimes it's hard to see examples of a healthy theology of biblical community. There is so much written in the New Testament on this topic that I am writing an entire other book about it and have not even scratched the surface. God has called us to be accountable to a local biblical community that points us to a vertical, intimate, abiding relationship with Christ and then provokes us to live in horizontal relationship with others.

Many people feel isolated in life and have felt ashamed or scared to share their pain and struggles with others. The family of God is just the opposite. The church should be the most transparent and authentic place around and should offer abundant grace and healing for everyone.

The phrase "one another," or *allelon* in Greek, is used over one hundred times in the New Testament in many different contexts.[18] One Greek word that is used many times in the New Testament about our fellowship with God and His church is *koinōnia*. This word means fellowship, communion, joint participation, contribution, sharing, or community.[19]

One of Satan's greatest tactics is to divide and isolate the people of God, and we must combat against it. Church is so much more than a simple gathering once a week. Church is a biblical community.

A Model for Biblical Community

In a church community, *koinonia*, we need each other, both in friendship and mentorship. We must be intentional in encouraging others in spiritual growth and conveying honesty about how we are growing and what we need.

The most effective model I have personally experienced is what I call the "Paul, Barnabas, Timothy model." These are characters from the early church whose stories we see in the New Testament. Every one of us needs all three types of people in our lives to help us become everything God has called us to be.

The Apostle Paul was the man God chose to write over half of the New Testament of the Bible. He was a leader, and he had an abiding relationship with Christ. Paul is an example of a spiritual leader in your life who will help you as you grow in your relationship with Christ. This person could be a pastor, mentor, or coach. Whoever it is should be further along spiritually than you are so he or she can help you with where you are going.

A Paul in your life could be an old friend or even a new one. He or she could be younger in age but older spiritually. Whoever it is should challenge you in your faith walk and be a consistent voice in your life that disciples you along the way. This person should be available for prayer, guidance, answering questions, and pointing you in the right direction to discover the answers you seek. He or she should be able to help you discover who God is and who you are in relationship with Him, as well as helping you to discover and grow in the gifts God has for you. What you call the Paul in your life is up to you. Many people use the term "spiritual father" or "spiritual mother." We see these terms used in the New Testament in response to older, more mature men and women discipling younger ones in the faith, like Paul did for Timothy. Notice how 1 Timothy begins:

> *Paul, an apostle of Jesus Christ, by the commandment of God our Savior and the Lord Jesus Christ, our hope,*
>
> *To Timothy, a true son in the faith....*
> **—1 Timothy 1:1–2**

Paul addressed Timothy as a "son in the faith." Paul clearly had a huge life investment and spiritual-fathering relationship with Timothy. In a different passage, Paul sent Timothy to the Philippian church as if he were an extension of himself:

> *But I trust in the Lord Jesus to send Timothy to you shortly, that I also may be encouraged when I know your state. For I have no one like-minded, who will sincerely care for your state. For all seek their own, not the things which are of Christ Jesus. But you know his proven character, that as a son with his father he served with me in the gospel.*
> **—Philippians 2:19–22**

It was not only Timothy, though. Look at how Paul described his relationship with some others in the Corinthian church:

I do not write these things to shame you, but as my beloved children I warn you. For though you might have ten thousand instructors in Christ, yet you do not have many fathers; for in Christ Jesus I have begotten you through the gospel. Therefore I urge you, imitate me. For this reason I have sent Timothy to you, who is my beloved and faithful son in the Lord, who will remind you of my ways in Christ, as I teach everywhere in every church.

—1 Corinthians 4:14–17

Clearly, Paul was a strong fathering voice and made many disciples. Prayerfully seek out someone in your life who can be a Paul to you on your relationship journey as you abide in Christ.

In Acts 9, we are introduced to Barnabas, who was a ministry partner and traveling companion to Paul. Who knows how differently Paul's ministry and life would have looked if he had not had a relationship with this man?

Barnabas was a catalyst in helping others to accept Paul when they thought that he was only pretending to be a Christian to arrest them. Barnabas is a great example of one who comes alongside others on their journey to help them get where they are going. His very name means "son of encouragement" (Acts 4:36). Having someone like Barnabas in your life is a very important relationship in which to invest.

We all need a person to offer accountability and encouragement in our daily walk. A Barnabas in your life should be one who is in the same place as you are spiritually. This person should be there to help you celebrate your victories and overcome your weaknesses. He or she should be available regularly to "do life" with you. When you leave your time with this person, you should feel uplifted, encouraged, and challenged.

As we saw above, Timothy was a son in the faith to the Apostle Paul. He was a young man of humility and meekness. Paul mentored Timothy and watched him develop into a godly man with spiritual integrity and character. Paul trusted Timothy like a son and poured his life into him so that Timothy could become all that he was meant to be. Timothy was commended in the Bible for being a man after Christ and faithful in his pursuit of the heart of God.

Timothy to you would be someone you could take under your wing and begin pouring your life into. You may not feel like the person to do this, but all that God is asking of you is your willingness and obedience. Don't worry or get ahead of yourself on this point. When you are ready, God will bring Timothys into your life for you to help, and you will know when that time comes.

If you are a parent, you have the sacred responsibility to be a Paul to your kids. They are Timothys to you. God has given us the institution of the family to raise children in discipleship of Christ. A good church will partner with the family to make disciples in the home. The church should not be the primary discipleship voice in your children's lives; you should be. You are not called to go be a Paul to others until you disciple the kids God gave you.

You must also learn to be a Timothy to others. If you are not careful in how you respond to a good leader in your life, you could easily push godly Pauls away from you. How you follow is just as important as whom you follow. Notice in the Scriptures how Paul talked about Timothy. He was full of humility, had a willingness to learn, and accepted being under accountability. Like Timothy, learn to be a teachable person and invite spiritually mature leaders to invest in you. Value their time and honor their wisdom.

God wants you in a local biblical community, where you can be accountable and hold others accountable. You are called to be an active participant in the body of Christ.

I want to conclude with a handful of verses that highlight the points we have made in this chapter:

And let us not grow weary while doing good, for in due season we shall reap if we do not lose heart. Therefore, as we have opportunity, let us do good to all, especially to those who are of the household of faith.

—Galatians 6:9–10

And let us consider one another in order to stir up love and good works, not forsaking the assembling of ourselves together, as is the manner of some, but exhorting one another, and so much the more as you see the Day approaching.

—Hebrews 10:24–25

As iron sharpens iron, so a man sharpens the countenance of his friend.

—Proverbs 27:17

Two are better than one, because they have a good reward for their labor. For if they fall, one will lift up his companion. But woe to him who is alone when he falls, for he has no one to help him up. Again, if two lie down together, they will keep warm; but how can one be warm alone? Though one may be overpowered by another, two can withstand him. And a threefold cord is not quickly broken.

—Ecclesiastes 4:9–12

I, therefore, the prisoner of the Lord, beseech you to walk worthy of the calling with which you were called, with all lowliness and gentleness, with longsuffering, bearing with one another in love, endeavoring to keep the unity of the

Spirit in the bond of peace. There is one body and one Spirit, just as you were called in one hope of your calling; one Lord, one faith, one baptism; one God and Father of all, who is above all, and through all, and in you all.

But to each one of us grace was given according to the measure of Christ's gift.

—Ephesians 4:1–7

Therefore if there is any consolation in Christ, if any comfort of love, if any fellowship of the Spirit, if any affection and mercy, fulfill my joy by being like-minded, having the same love, being of one accord, of one mind. Let nothing be done through selfish ambition or conceit, but in lowliness of mind let each esteem others better than himself. Let each of you look out not only for his own interests, but also for the interests of others.

—Philippians 2:1–4

God has placed you in His body as an individual and an important part. The body of Christ is not complete without your participation. I encourage you to steward what God has given you by investing in your local church body. Be a Paul, a Barnabas, and a Timothy. Be a disciple of Christ and go and make disciples.

WORKBOOK

Chapter Seven Questions

Question: Who is a Paul in your life, a mentor or spiritual parent who can disciple you and teach you to live an abiding life? If you do not already have a Paul in your life, ask God to lead you to one. Are you ready to be a Timothy? What does it mean to be teachable?

_____

_____

_____

_____

_____

_____

_____

_____

_____

_____

Question: Who can you do life with within your church or the greater Christian community? (Many churches have small groups set up for this purpose. Ask your pastor for help in locating one if you are not sure.) Who offers you encouragement and accountability? How can you offer encouragement to others as well? What are some of the sacrifices of time and transparency necessary to have Barnabas relationships?

_____

_____

_____

_____

_____

_____

_____

_____

_____

_____

Action: Research some ways parents can disciple their children. If you have children at home, how can you move from being just a physical parent to a spiritual one? If this idea is new to you, talk to some parents who are actively discipling their families about how to model and teach an abiding relationship with Christ.

_____

_____

_____

_____

_____

_____

_____

_____

_____

_____

_____

_____

Journal: Use the STAR journal process to learn the principles of community in Hebrews 10:24–25. How can you apply these verses to your Paul, Barnabas, and Timothy relationships?

Chapter Seven Notes

CHAPTER EIGHT

God's Blueprint for Your Life

Do you know that your life matters and that God has a plan and purpose for your life? You are here for a purpose, and that purpose is divine. Most people don't realize or don't believe that the God of the entire universe cares anything for them. We feel so insignificant in the big scheme of things. God is amazing. He is the Ruler of the universe. He is so far beyond our comprehension that it can hurt your head if you try to fathom His vastness. That is what makes His desire to have fellowship with you so great. He looks past everything else in eternity and spends one-on-one time with each of His children. He is an amazing Father.

God is not a faceless deity. He has been intimately involved in human history. He created you the way you are and needs you to be that person. I call this God's blueprint. A blueprint is a detailed outline or plan of action. Part of your walk with God is the revelation of His blueprint for your life. As you grow in God, you discover the uniqueness of His design for your life. God created you special and has given you gifts that are special to you. He needs you to be you. If two of us are identical, then one of us is unnecessary. God did not make us robots, with all the same functions.

If you follow the blueprint that God lays out for you, then you will have a simple, clarified plan of action that will produce eternal success. Make some time to read through Psalm 139. This chapter is a powerful reminder that God knows each of us intimately and has a plan for our lives that involves His purposes. Each one of us is "fearfully and wonderfully made" (Psalm 139:14), which tells us that God's blueprints for our lives are tailored to our own special gifts and talents.

A Simple Blueprint in Verse

The following passage is my favorite one in the Bible because it lays out the fact of God's blueprint for each individual's life:

> But the end of all things is at hand; therefore be serious and watchful in your prayers. And above all things have fervent love for one another, for "love will cover a multitude of sins." Be hospitable to one another without grumbling. As each one has received a gift, minister it to one another, as good stewards of the manifold grace of God. If anyone speaks, let him speak as the oracles of God. If anyone ministers, let him do it as with the ability which God supplies, that in all things God may be glorified through Jesus Christ, to whom belong the glory and the dominion forever and ever. Amen.
>
> **—1 Peter 4:7–11**

First, "be serious and watchful in your prayers" (1 Peter 4:7). Prayer feeds your abiding fellowship with Christ. In times of prayer, God will speak vision and destiny for your life.

Second, we must love and possess a fervent love. If we have fervent love for one another as a fruit of our abiding in Christ, then it will cover a multitude of failures and shortfalls that each of us experiences. Instead of criticism and competition, we should walk in love as it pertains to our relationships. This covering of love will produce an environment of support and celebration for each other. *Third, this passage clearly states that each one of us has received a gift from God.* This does not just apply to the pastor or the super-holy people. God has given you a gift. Say that to yourself right now: "I have received a gift from God." This gift is to be used for ministry. What I am saying is that you are called to be a minister for God. Too many churches believe that the minister is the pastor in the pulpit, preaching the message, but the Bible says that we all are ministers. You must get it into the depths of your soul that *you* are a minister for God.

You are to take this gift and minister it as a good steward. A steward is someone who manages the goods or property of someone else. God requires you to use the gift He gave you, and He will hold you accountable for how you did. As you read this, your insecurities and fear may be trying to creep in because you don't feel like you have what it takes to be a minister for God. Well, join the club. Fear, insecurity, or pride is no excuse to avoid being a minister.

We read in 1 Peter 4:11 that we are to minister "with the ability which God supplies." It's His ability in you that makes you able to do whatever He asks you to do. If you were to do it in your own ability or confidence, you would not need faith in Him and, therefore, would not give Him glory for it. God deserves the glory and wants your life to bring Him glory. This happens when you yield your will to Him and, in obedience, minister how He created you to minister.

As you minister, one pitfall you might experience is comparison. Don't compare yourself with anyone else. God usually does not call you to do something that is easy for you or doesn't require faith in Him. He wants the glory and will stretch you to do things for Him that are beyond your capability so that no one but He can claim the credit. God uses ordinary people to do extraordinary things so that He always gets the glory! This is the end result of living a life in complete abiding with Christ according to the blueprint He has for us. There are four key principles of a godly blueprint that we would do well to keep in mind as we continue to minister to others and live abundant lives in Christ.

Four Principles of a Godly Blueprint

1. A godly blueprint is God-breathed. You must receive your blueprint directly from God, "being confident of this very thing, that He who has begun a good work in you will complete it until the day of Jesus Christ" (Philippians 1:6). If you want to have success in life and bring Him glory, you must submit to His blueprint, "for of Him and through Him and to Him are all things, to whom be glory forever. Amen" (Romans 11:36). This is why abiding is so important. Hearing His voice and allowing Him to lead you according to His plans is crucial for lasting fruit.

2. A godly blueprint is God-empowered. It's easy to start a race or a journey. There are many people at the starting gate, but there are few at the finish line. Paul wrote these encouraging words: "And let us not grow weary while doing good, for in due season we shall reap if we do not lose heart" (Galatians 6:9). We read in Isaiah 40:31 that "those who wait on the LORD shall renew their strength; they shall mount up with wings like eagles, they shall run and not be weary, they shall walk and not faint."

If you want to have success in God's kingdom, you have to allow Him to empower you to reach the finish line. It is easy to get off and tell God that you've got it from here and don't need Him. This will leave you laboring in your own strength and ability. Other times, you will get distracted and off course. Allow God to be the leader and follow His blueprint closely so you don't grow weary and disqualify yourself from the race.

3. A godly blueprint is God-fulfilled. Disciples allow God to author their faith and, through abiding in Christ, give Him permission to be the finisher of their faith:

> *Therefore we also, since we are surrounded by so great a cloud of witnesses, let us lay aside every weight, and the sin which so easily ensnares us, and let us run with endurance the race that is set before us, looking unto Jesus, the author and finisher of our faith, who for the joy that was set before Him endured the cross, despising the shame, and has sat down at the right hand of the throne of God.*
> **—Hebrews 12:1-2**

If you are going to navigate God's blueprint successfully, you must allow Him to bring the fulfillment. Do you trust that God knows what He is doing and that He can do it better than you can? Of course He can. Let God bring the fulfillment of His plan for your life.

If it is of God, then it will usually be beyond your scope of completion anyway. He will put you in hopeless situations so you will rely on Him, and when He delivers you, it will be accompanied by the miraculous. If you believe that He authored your blueprint, then why would you try to be the finisher? Let God make it happen.

4. A godly blueprint is God-glorifying. God's blueprint for your life is not about your happiness or your comfort. It comes down to one thing: bringing Him glory, "that in all things God may be glorified through Jesus Christ, to whom belong the glory and the dominion forever and ever. Amen" (1 Peter 4:11).

God's blueprint for your life is not about you. God does

not do what He does to make you comfortable. The quicker you realize that your life is about bringing Him glory, the sooner you will be able to walk out the blueprint He has for you. Allow God to be glorified in every part of your daily life. Pointing people to Him will bring you great joy and peace.

WORKBOOK

Chapter Eight Questions

Question: What plans have you had for your life, from your childhood dreams to your teenage ambitions and young adult decisions? Does the thought of God authoring and finishing the blueprint of your life fill you with excitement or anxiety? Are you surrendered to His plan, or do you want to control the direction and choose the details? How do you know that His path is better than any you could choose?

_____

_____

_____

_____

_____

_____

_____

_____

_____

_____

_____

Question: Who is someone you know or know of whom God has used far beyond human expectations or abilities? How can you demonstrate your dependence on God to lead you, transform you, and use you beyond your own strength and talent? Are you more concerned with God's glory or your own? How can you keep His glory your desire and focus?

_____

_____

_____

_____

_____

_____

_____

_____

_____

_____

_____

Action: Do a study on spiritual gifts. There are many excellent resources to help you with discovering your spiritual gift and learning how you can use it to minister for God. Ask your pastor or spiritual mentor to help you evaluate how God has gifted you and find ways you can begin putting that gift to use in the church.

_____

_____

_____

_____

_____

_____

_____

_____

_____

_____

Journal: Use the STAR journal process to study 1 Peter 4:7–11. What does this passage teach you about God's blueprint for your life?

Chapter Eight Notes

CONCLUSION

Knowing Christ and Making Him Known

I pray that this book has been an amazing time for you as you pursue the God of the universe. I assume that there have been some thoughts and emotions that have left you feeling like you just walked off of a roller coaster, while others have brought your heart comfort and peace. I want to set your mind at ease and give you a simple process to follow that will make it easier to stay on a good path moving forward. There is much learning and growing ahead, and I want to help you stay focused on the main thing, which is Christ.

As you spend time in church and around the church world, there may be a tendency to complicate things. Many Christians fall into the trap of thinking that more is better. They will try to convince you that you need Christ and then try to add things on top of Christ for your salvation. Many of these people are good-hearted, but they can lead you astray from abiding.

Jesus kept things very simple and spoke practically to people. So many times, the simplicity of Christ's method is judged as being too easy. People think that there must

be more to it: "Give me something to do, and I'll do it."
Do not lose fellowship with Him in your efforts to know
about Him. The most important thing moving forward is
your abiding in Him. This should never be overrun in your
pursuit of knowledge about God. There is a big difference,
and it is easy to fall into this trap.

I encourage you to make the following statement your
life mission and motto: *knowing Christ and making Him
known*. If you wake up every day with this as your focus,
then you will stay in an abiding relationship with Christ
and make His focus yours. What you do for God will
change on a regular basis as He reveals to you more of the
blueprint for your life, but your fellowship with Him
should never change.

Knowing Christ is crucial for living a successful
Christian life. Part of being a Christ follower is making
Him known. You will not do this if you don't have a
personal, abiding relationship with Him. People recognize
authenticity. If you are trying to share about a God with
whom you do not have fellowship, people will see that
from a mile away. That is religion. You have a form of
God but deny the power to live for Him every day (2
Timothy 3:5).

When you make it your life's mission to know Christ,
making Him known will be a natural outflow and fruit of
your relationship with Him. You won't have to muster up
the energy to share your faith. The gospel will just flow
out of you, and people will recognize the authenticity of
that.

I want to share with you a simple process that gives
you practical steps to fulfill this new-found life's motto of
knowing Christ and making Him known. This is not a
step-by-step program that will help you to arrive at a
spiritual plateau and be done with it. This process is never-
ending; it revolves on a daily basis, keeping you in
proximity to Christ. This process will help to keep you

close to Christ while, at the same time, sharing His love with others.

Experience, Grow, Share

Experience. Every day, you should find ways to experience Christ as you go about your business. This can happen in a time of prayer, worship, or devotion or in a whole host of other ways. It should not be limited to a time frame set apart in your day. You should learn to experience Him all day, every day.

Abiding in Christ takes a big commitment. There are many things fighting for your time, and the tyranny of the urgent usually wins out. You must make Him a priority and include Him in every part of your day. Remember that Christ should be the center of your life instead of just at the top of a list for the day.

If I were only to speak to my wife once a week at church, our relationship would be strained over time. I would stop experiencing her. In much the same way, many Christians think that they can experience Christ once a week in an hour-long church service. This limited time will slowly stress the relationship. You will quit abiding in Him and will only go to Him on your terms when you want something. You will quit hearing His leading, and His blueprint will slowly fade away until you are living your life for yourself again. This is a slippery slope that many Christians fall down.

And this is eternal life, that they may know You, the only true God, and Jesus Christ whom You have sent.
—John 17:3

...that I may know Him and the power of His resurrection,

and the fellowship of His sufferings, being conformed to His death....

—Philippians 3:10

There are several ways to experience God throughout the day. Make your drive to work a time of abiding. Acknowledge Christ in your work and make your work worship of Him. Washing dishes can be a time of worship and communion with Him. Folding laundry can be surrounded with the presence of God. Are you getting it now? Make it a commitment to experience Him all day, every day.

Grow. This part of the process involves discovery and growing in every way possible. Discover who God is and who you are in relationship with Him. Discover your purpose, what He has created you to be and to do, as He unfolds it to you over the next seasons of your life. Grow in the gifts that God has given you. Grow in fellowship with Him. Grow in the knowledge of the Word. Grow in your faith. Grow in His love for you. Grow in your stewardship of His gifts. Grow in your connection with your biblical community. Every day, you should find practical ways to develop in your relationship with God.

This could involve a daily Bible study, a church discipleship class, leading your family in devotions, or many other things. The more you can learn about God and the Bible, with Him, the more He can grow you and lead you according to His will. This has to happen alongside experiencing Him. You don't want to gain knowledge without relationship. However, when the two work hand in hand, you will see God reveal things to you that you never comprehended before.

...but grow in the grace and knowledge of our Lord and Savior Jesus Christ. To Him be the glory both now and

forever. Amen.

—*2 Peter 3:18*

But as it is written: "Eye has not seen, nor ear heard, nor have entered into the heart of man the things which God has prepared for those who love Him."

But God has revealed them to us through His Spirit. For the Spirit searches all things, yes, the deep things of God.

—*1 Corinthians 2:9–10*

So many believers find Christ and let Him be their Savior who provides an escape from hell. They stop there and don't allow God to be their Lord. There is a big difference. When Christ is your Lord, you are growing every day toward personal abandonment and absolute trust in Him. You experience eternal life here and now, not just in heaven.

Share. This part of the process involves sharing the love of Christ in practical ways. When you experience and grow in God every day, sharing Him will be a natural outflow of your life.

You will find ways to share His love with people in your area of influence. There are people God has placed in your life who may never hear the message of Christ outside of your sharing it with them. This is a responsibility and a privilege. Remember that your life is about bringing glory to God. What better way to bring Him glory than to share your story of how God's love transformed your life so others know that He can do the same for them?

God will give you divine appointments with people and open doors simply to talk about Him. You can use this process to share His love. It's less about Scripture verses and theology and more about letting them know that God loves them and wants to be in relationship with them.

I want to warn you, though, that sharing the love of Christ becomes addictive. When you share His love and someone comes to know Him, it is the most awesome experience on earth! Heaven rejoices, and you get excited to share Him with even more people. Paul wrote:

So, as much as is in me, I am ready to preach the gospel to you who are in Rome also.

For I am not ashamed of the gospel of Christ, for it is the power of God to salvation for everyone who believes, for the Jew first and also for the Greek.
—Romans 1:15–16

Thank you for allowing this book to speak into your new season and possibly act as a catalyst to help you know Christ and make Him known. God has wonderful things ahead for you as you walk with Him and remain in Him. The most important thing you could ever learn on this earth is to abide in Christ because this will transform everything in your life and give you an eternal perspective and purpose.

WORKBOOK

Conclusion Questions

Question: Do you have a mission statement or motto for your life? What are some of your favorite purpose statements? Does the phrase "knowing Christ and making Him known" reflect the desire of your heart? What are some ways you can do this, starting today?

_____

_____

_____

_____

_____

_____

_____

_____

_____

_____

Question: List some practical ways you can incorporate knowing Christ into your daily life. When do you have downtime? To what mental defaults do you turn? How much time do you spend on social media, watching television, playing video games, surfing the web, or otherwise mentally checking out, and how could this time be redeemed for Christ? What is a decision you could take today that would move you from self-focus to Christ-focus in the day-in, day-out activities of your life?

_____

_____

_____

_____

_____

_____

_____

_____

_____

_____

_____

Action: Making Christ known can be intimidating if you have never shared the gospel with another person, but there are many resources to guide you. Take a class, read a book, or go with a mentor to learn how to share your faith. Allow these things to help you, not to replace the Holy Spirit's prompting and supernatural work through you. Then pray for and plan an opportunity to make Christ known. Meet with an unsaved friend or take part in a church's mission initiative.

_____

_____

_____

_____

_____

_____

_____

_____

_____

_____

_____

_____

Journal: Choose one verse under each category of *experience*, *grow*, and *share*. Journal about it using the STAR method. How have the Scripture verses and content in this book changed you and given you direction in your walk with Christ?

Conclusion Notes

_____

_____

_____

_____

_____

_____

_____

_____

_____

_____

_____

_____

_____

_____

_____

_____

_____

_____

_____

_____

_____

_____

APPENDIX A

Journaling 101
by Rocky Fleming

On your journey to intimacy with Christ, one thing that can greatly assist you is journaling. This is a foreign concept to most people. However, journaling can be a gift from God to you. Many times, we learn to internalize our thoughts, keeping them hidden in the deep recesses of our minds. Journaling is a way to help you get those issues out of your heart and onto the altar before God.

In this technological age of high-speed communication, written words have been lost. Today, most of our thoughts and reflections about life—if they even make it out of our heads—are condensed into brief digital formats, which are then deleted in cyberspace before they have a chance to sink into our consciousness. There is power in the written word on paper. God wants us to slow down and be still for a few moments with Him, and just like He instructed countless people from Moses to Paul, He wants us to write down the revelations He gives us.

In the pages of this book, there is a lot of information for you to navigate prayerfully. We have included this simple form of journaling to help you put down on paper some key things that may be speaking the loudest to you. When you write things down, there is a tendency to remember more and create further action steps to implement the learning pieces. If you are going to invest the time to read this book, it would greatly benefit you to utilize journaling through the workbook section at the end of each chapter. If you are inspired to become an abiding leader of an abiding church, there will be much to process, and this method can help you to simplify this.

STAR Journaling Exercise Template

#1 Scripture Read/Promise Given/Question Asked

Read the verse and/or question and walk through the STAR/SPAR process. Pause and prayerfully meditate on what is being said, read, or asked.

#2 Thought Conveyed/Promise Given

In this part, write down what this means to you so that you can clearly understand the question, Scripture, thought, or promise. Make it personal to get the most out of it.

#3 Application Made

How does this teaching apply to me right now? How does this apply to my leadership context?

#4 Response Given

What can I do immediately to apply this to my life? How should I respond/react to this promise or instruction? What are some long-term things I need to respond to?

Used with permission from Rocky Fleming and www.Influencers.org.[20]

APPENDIX B

Further Resources

The Journey is a nine- to twelve-month process, with most groups meeting every other week. It is divided into three main segments called Enlightened, Enabled, and Expressing.

The Enlightened segment of the Journey is the foundation of the process. The step-by-step understanding of the four personal aspects of God ("He Knows," "He Cares," "He Is Willing," and "He Is Able") is designed to help the participants realize that God is a loving, caring, and intimate God, who wants to involve Himself in every area of their lives. This new understanding should guide the participants to the goal of being willing to trust God with their lives and should prepare the way for the second segment of the Journey.

The Enabled segment of the Journey focuses on an abiding, intimate relationship with Jesus. This segment helps the participants to understand how the Holy Spirit enables them to develop this new level of intimacy. The participants are guided through an understanding of the "fruit of the Spirit" and how this fruit enables the use of the "gifts of the Spirit." This should help each of the participants to better understand his or her role and purpose in the work of God's kingdom. Above all else, the Enabled segment should guide the participants toward the goal of releasing control of their lives and experiencing the joy of personal abandonment found in an abiding relationship with Jesus.

The Expressing segment of the Journey is the culmination of the Journey process. The principles of "Being a God Seeker," "Being a God Abider," and "Live It Out" are used as the guide to help the participants fully understand the entire Journey. The participants are introduced to the concept of servant leadership within marriage, the family, and the world around them. They are challenged to grasp the concept of "blooming where they are planted" and being ready to partner with God to influence the world in a supernatural way. At the end of the Journey, the participants are released to take the name "Influencer" and begin to bear fruit that lasts by expressing Christlike love to all those around them.

The Journey experience has three main components for each participant.

The first is a personal "treasure hunt" conducted during the days between sessions. This is the core of the Journey and the place where heart transformation takes place. This "treasure hunt" guides the participant toward the "Inner Chamber," where intimacy with Christ is discovered and experienced.

The second component is one-on-one time between the guide and the participant. This individual time is critical to the participant's journey as the guide and the participant share their life stories.

The third component is the group sessions, which are designed to give the group opportunities to discuss their journey and share discovered truth. Each session enhances the other two components and ties the Journey together.

This Journey process will lay a strong foundation that you can build upon as you pursue your long-term growth track.

Influencers is a ministry with the goal of guiding people into an intimate, abiding relationship with Jesus Christ. They accomplish this through Journey groups, who journey together for nine months, desiring a closer proximity to the Father. Participants discover God in a most personal way through Scripture, journaling, group discussion, prayer, and study materials.

Jesus said, "I am the vine; you are the branches. If you remain in me and I in you, you will bear much fruit; apart from me you can do nothing" (John 15:5 NIV). For years, good Christian people have been striving to bear fruit for God. However, they have missed the part about "remaining in Him." Influencers help people to press the pause button in life so that they can take time to seek Jesus and find renewed hope and purpose.

Thousands of people—increasingly including women and married couples—have gone on this Journey worldwide, and thousands more are finding their way to this life-giving process. If you would like to know more about Influencers and the Journey and how to start a group in your city, go to the website at www.influencers.org.

Other Resources

- *I'm a Catalyst* membership manual by Catalyst Church
- *The Abiding Church: Creating, Cultivating, and Stewarding a Culture of Discipleship* by Nate Sweeney
- *Abiding at the Feet of Jesus: A Study on the Beatitudes* by Nate Sweeney
- *Abiding in Identity: Who I Am Because of Whose I Am* by Nate Sweeney
- *Journey to the Inner Chamber* by Rocky Fleming
- *Knowing Christ and Making Him Known* by Nate Sweeney
- *5-2-1 Leadership Planning*

APPENDIX C

The Abiding Network Doctrines

These are the doctrines of The Abiding Network:

1. *The Church*: God's kingdom (Matthew 16:18; 1 Corinthians 3:16). We believe that we are the church and God's kingdom on the earth. We are to be the expression of His love and produce fruits of righteousness through the Holy Spirit housed in us. Jesus is the Chief Shepherd and Senior Pastor. He said that He would build His church, and we strive to follow Him in that. First Peter 2:9–10 says (about the church) that "you are a chosen generation, a royal priesthood, a holy nation, His own special people, that you may proclaim the praises of Him who called you out of darkness into His marvelous light; who once were not a people but are now the people of God, who had not obtained mercy but now have obtained mercy."

2. *God's Word*: The Scriptures. The Bible is the inspired Word of God. It is the product of holy men of old who spoke and wrote as they were moved by the Holy Spirit. We accept the new covenant, as recorded in the New Testament, as our infallible guide in matters pertaining to conduct and doctrine. (2 Timothy 3:16; 1

Thessalonians 2:13; 2 Peter 1:21)

3. *The Law of Moses—the Law of Love.* We believe that God gave the Law to: show humanity their sin; produce brokenness and the realization that there is nothing you can do in and of yourself to fix the sin that is revealed; and drive you to Christ and the experience of His love, grace, and acceptance (Romans 3:20; Galatians 3:23–25; Matthew 5:21–23). We believe that Jesus expressed the heart of God when He summed up the Law with Matthew 22:36–40:

> *"Teacher, which is the great commandment in the law?"*
> *Jesus said to him, "'You shall love the LORD your God with all your heart, with all your soul, and with all your mind.'*
> *This is the first and great commandment. And the second is like it: 'You shall love your neighbor as yourself.' On these two commandments hang all the Law and the Prophets."*

4. *God Exists*: The Godhead. Our God is one, but manifested in three Persons—the Father, the Son, and the Holy Spirit, being coequal (Deuteronomy 6:4; Philippians 2:6). God the Father is greater than all, the Sender of the Word (*Logos*) and the Begetter (John 14:28; John 16:28; John 1:14). The Son is the Word flesh-covered, the One Begotten, and has existed with the Father from the beginning (John 1:1; John 1:18; John 1:14). The Holy Spirit proceeds forth from both the Father and the Son and is eternal (John 14:16; John 15:26). God has a plan and purpose for each person's life and desires relationship, fellowship, and intimacy with us.

5. *Original Sin*: Man is a created being, made in the likeness and image of God, but through Adam's transgression and fall, sin came into the world. The Bible says that "all have sinned and fall short of the glory of

God" (Romans 3:23) and that "there is none righteous, no, not one" (Romans 3:10b). Jesus Christ, the Son of God, was manifested to undo the works of the devil. He gave His life and shed His blood to redeem and restore man back to God (Romans 5:14; 1 John 3:8). Salvation is the gift of God to man, separate from works and the Law, and is made operative by grace through faith in Jesus Christ, producing works acceptable to God (Ephesians 2:8–10).

6. *Justification Through Faith and Eternal Life*: The New-Birth Man's first step toward salvation is godly sorrow that brings repentance. The New Birth is necessary for all men and, when experienced, produces eternal life (2 Corinthians 7:10; John 3:3–5; 1 John 5:12). Eternal life is to be experienced through relationship with God in this life and will continue into eternity.

7. *Transformed and Renewed*: The Bible teaches that without Holiness no man can see the Lord. We believe that at salvation, there is a definite heart change and we are reconciled to God. The Holy Spirit does a re-creative work, and we are born again. We are empowered for godly living through the Holy Spirit. We believe that there is a definite and progressive process of transformation, sanctification, and renewal of the mind that will change us incrementally into the image of God until the consummation of salvation at Christ's return. (Romans 12:1–2; Hebrews 12:14; 1 Thessalonians 5:23; 2 Peter 3:18; 2 Corinthians 3:17–18; Philippians 3:12–14; 1 Corinthians 1:30)

8. *Repentance and Baptism*: We believe that godly repentance will lead us to leave a lifestyle of sin to pursue righteousness with God. Many times, Jesus and others associated baptism with repentance. Water baptism is an outward declaration and celebration of an inward work of repentance. Baptism in water, by immersion, is a direct commandment of our Lord and is for believers only. The

ordinance is a symbol of the Christian's identification with Christ in His death, burial, and resurrection. (Matthew 28:19; Romans 6:4; Colossians 2:12; Acts 8:36–39)

The following recommendation regarding the water baptismal formula is adopted: "On the confession of your faith in the Lord Jesus Christ, the Son of God, and by His authority, I baptize you in the Name of the Father, and the Son, and the Holy Ghost. Amen."

9. *Heaven and Hell*: We believe in the resurrection of both the lost and the saved: the lost into eternal damnation and separation from God, the saved into eternal life in the presence of God. Jesus said:

Let not your heart be troubled; you believe in God, believe also in Me. In My Father's house are many mansions; if it were not so, I would have told you. I go to prepare a place for you. And if I go and prepare a place for you, I will come again and receive you to Myself; that where I am, there you may be also.

—John 14:1–3

His coming is imminent (John 14:1–4; Acts 1:11; 1 Thessalonians 4:16–17). The one who physically dies in his sins without accepting Christ is hopelessly and eternally lost in the lake of fire and, therefore, has no further opportunity of hearing the gospel or repenting. The lake of fire is literal. The terms *eternal* and *everlasting* used in describing the duration of the punishment of the damned in the lake of fire carry the same thought and meaning of endless existence as they do when used in denoting the duration of joy and ecstasy of saints in the presence of God. (Hebrews 9:27; Revelation 19:20)

10. *Communion—The Lord's Supper*: We partake of

the Lord's Supper to show the Lord's death till He comes (1 Corinthians 11:23–31). The bread symbolizes the Lord's broken body (Isaiah 53:5; 1 Corinthians 11:24). The cup represents the new covenant in His blood, which provides us with forgiveness and relationship with God (Hebrews 9; 1 Corinthians 11:25). We judge ourselves and realize that this is our salvation and receive it (1 Corinthians 11:28–30), for if we receive it unworthily, without giving it honor as our salvation, we are guilty of the body and the blood of the Lord (1 Corinthians 11:27).

11. *Empowered by the Spirit*: We believe that all the fruit and gifts of the Holy Spirit, explained in the New Testament, are available and in operation in the body of Christ today. Jesus declared in Acts 1:8 that we need to be empowered to be His witnesses to the world. Jesus said that the Holy Spirit would be with us and in us. This empowerment is accompanied by many outward manifestations and signs that Jesus said would follow those who believe. (1 Corinthians 12; Mark 16:15–20; Acts 1:8; Acts 2:1–4; Galatians 5:22; John 14:16–18; John 16:12–15)

12. *The Great Commission*: We believe that Jesus commands us to go and share the good news of His love for humanity. Our daily lives are a mission to introduce and reconcile people to God. Everything we are as believers should come from the love of God that transformed our lives. Everything we do as believers should center on the Great Commission fueled by His love in our transformed hearts. (Matthew 28:18–20; Mark 16:15–20; John 20:21–22; 2 Corinthians 5:17–18)

About the Author

Nate Sweeney would be considered an average person, someone who loves his family, community, and church. The major factor that sets him apart is his passion to Know Christ and Make Him Known. This vision is at the forefront of Nate's daily focus and drives him to stay connected to Christ and share that relationship with others. Nate pursues this vision in his home with his wife, Monica, and their three kids.

Nate has served in many ministry capacities since he graduated from Bible school in 1997. He is the directional leader of Catalyst Church in Bentonville, Arkansas. Nate is the founder and directional leader of The Abiding

Network, and he sits on the Influencers Ministry global board as a church relations leader.

Nate speaks with experience, as he has led his church to be transformed into an Abiding Church, and his role has become supported by the great leaders who have been raised up in this church. At the time of this publishing, Nate has mentored, coached, and helped to disciple hundreds of church leaders nationally.

It is evident through Nate's ministry that people are challenged to experience God daily and grow in their relationship with Him, while discovering what He has called them to do in life and sharing His love in practical ways.

About Sermon To Book

SermonToBook.com began with a simple belief: that sermons should be touching lives, *not* collecting dust. That's why we turn sermons into high-quality books that are accessible to people all over the globe.

Turning your sermon series into a book exposes more people to God's Word, better equips you for counseling, accelerates future sermon prep, adds credibility to your ministry, and even helps make ends meet during tight times.

John 21:25 tells us that the world itself couldn't contain the books that would be written about the work of Jesus Christ. Our mission is to try anyway. Because in heaven, there will no longer be a need for sermons or books. Our time is now.

If God so leads you, we'd love to work with you on your sermon or sermon series.

Visit www.sermontobook.com to learn more.

REFERENCES

Notes

1 Sweeney, Nate. "Knowing Christ and Making Him Known." YouVersion. https://www.bible.com/reading-plans/14952-knowing-christ-making-him-known.

2 Fleming, Rocky. "Journaling." Influencers Global Ministries. www.influencers.org/journaling.

3 Herrick, Greg. "Understanding the Meaning of the Term 'Disciple.'" *Go and Make Disciples of All Nations*. Bible.org. May 11, 2014. https://bible.org/seriespage/2-understanding-meaning-term-disciple.

4 *Dictionary.com*, "convert." Based on *Random House Unabridged Dictionary*. Random House, 2020. https://www.dictionary.com/browse/convert?s=t.

5 *Blue Letter Bible*, "G1319 – didaskalia." https://www.blueletterbible.org/lang/lexicon/lexicon.cfm?t=kjv&strongs=g1319.

6 Strong, James. "G3875: parakletos." *A Concise Dictionary of*

the Words in the Greek Testament and the Hebrew Bible. Faithlife, 2019.

[7] Strong, James. "G1411: dunamis." *A Concise Dictionary of the Words in the Greek Testament and the Hebrew Bible.* Faithlife, 2019.

[8] *Blue Letter Bible*, "G4137 – plēroō." https://www.blueletter bible.org/lang/lexicon/lexicon.cfm?t=kjv&strongs=g4137.

[9] *Blue Letter Bible*, "G5485 – charis." https://www.blueletter bible.org/lang/lexicon/lexicon.cfm?t=KJV&strongs=g5485.

[10] *Blue Letter Bible*, "G5486 – charisma." https://www. blueletterbible.org/lang/lexicon/lexicon.cfm?t=kjv&strongs=g 5486.

[11] *Blue Letter Bible*, "G5545 – chrisma." https://www.blueletter bible.org/lang/lexicon/lexicon.cfm?t=kjv&strongs=g5545.

[12] Thomas, R. L. *New American Standard Hebrew-Aramaic and Greek Dictionaries.* Updated edition. Foundation Publications, 1998.

[13] *Dictionary.com*, "repent." Based on *Random House Unabridged Dictionary.* Random House, 2020. https://www.dictionary.com/browse/repent?s=t.

[14] *Dictionary.com*, "repent."

[15] *Dictionary.com*, "conformed." Based on *Random House Unabridged Dictionary.* Random House, 2020. https://www.dictionary.com/browse/conformed.

[16] Grady, J. Lee. "How Billy Graham Avoided Scandal His Entire Life." Charisma News. March 1, 2010. https://www.charismanews.com/opinion/69841-how-billy-

---

graham-avoided-scandal-his-entire-life.

[17] *Dictionary.com*, "transformation." Based on *Random House Unabridged Dictionary*. Random House, 2020. https://www.dictionary.com/browse/transformation.

[18] *Blue Letter Bible*, "G240 – allelon." https://www.blueletterbible.org/lang/lexicon/lexicon.cfm?Strongs=G240&t=NKJV.

[19] Strong, James. "G2842: koinoia." *A Concise Dictionary of the Words in the Greek Testament and The Hebrew Bible.* Faithlife, 2019.

[20] Rocky Fleming, "Journaling."

Made in the USA
Monee, IL
16 July 2020

36301694R10085